DATE

The Influence Agenda

A Systematic Approach to
Aligning Stakeholders in
Times of Change

The Influence Agenda

Mike Clayton

First published 2014 by
PALGRAVE MACMILLAN

Palgrave Macmillan in the UK is an imprint of Macmillan Publishers Limited, registered in England, company number 785998, of Houndmills, Basingstoke, Hampshire RG21 6XS.

Palgrave Macmillan in the US is a division of St Martin's Press LLC, 175 Fifth Avenue, New York, NY 10010.

Palgrave Macmillan is the global academic imprint of the above companies and has companies and representatives throughout the world.

Palgrave® and Macmillan® are registered trademarks in the United States, the United Kingdom, Europe and other countries.

ISBN 978–1–137–35584–3

This book is printed on paper suitable for recycling and made from fully managed and sustained forest sources. Logging, pulping and manufacturing processes are expected to conform to the environmental regulations of the country of origin.

A catalogue record for this book is available from the British Library.

A catalog record for this book is available from the Library of Congress.

Typeset by MPS Limited, Chennai, India.

The Influence Agenda *is dedicated to a former friend and colleague, Judith Wilks. Judith had a deep intuitive understanding of the contents of this book; things I have had to learn the hard way. Judith died after a long struggle with cancer in early 2012.*

Contents

List of Figures

List of Tables

List of Templates

Acknowledgements

Throughout *The Influence Agenda* are case studies and 'wise words' that were generously provided to me by former colleagues. Whilst I have a learned a lot from many of the colleagues and clients I have worked with, thank you particularly to Colin Bartle-Tubbs, Paul Mitchell, Carolyn Pratley and Charles Vivian, who all took time out of their busy schedules to speak with me and review the notes I made. Their experience and wisdom has added significantly to this book. I would also like to make a posthumous acknowledgement of the many conversations I had with Judith Wilks, to whom this book is dedicated, while we worked together.

Other colleagues and clients whose knowledge and expertise I particularly benefited from include: Julian Badcock, Tricia Bey, Brian Green, George Owen, Richard Porter, Ron Rosenhead, Steve Shergold, Chris Sullivan, Gilbert Toppin and Nick Wilson.

Finally, thank you again to my wife, Felicity, for her constant indulgence of my commitment to writing and for her continuing willingness to read yet another manuscript.

Why You Need *The Influence Agenda*

Do you need to make change happen?

If you do, you probably have a wide range of different people to deal with in the process. Some will be natural supporters of what you are trying to achieve, but others may oppose you. Some will have strong opinions about what you are doing and how you should go about it, while others will adopt a wait-and-see approach. You will find people who are affected profoundly by what you are doing, yet say nothing, while some will make a ruckus, despite having little to do with you.

Project management and the leadership of change are tough enough at the best of times, but it is the varying demands, opinions and attitudes of the people you will come across in the process that will make them harder still. The hardest thing of all is the soft stuff.

Most project management books and books on change will talk about the need to manage stakeholders – the people who are affected by your project. And books on change management will cover how to prepare people for change and take them with you. But if you aspire to practise project management or lead change at a high level, all the while honing your skills, neither of these will be enough: this is the gap into which *The Influence Agenda* steps.

What you will get

The Influence Agenda does five things. After reading it, you will be able to:

1. chart a clear path for the process of engaging and influencing your stakeholders;

2. confidently identify your stakeholders and understand what drives their choices and how to prioritise them accurately;
3. build structured communication programmes and craft messages that influence and persuade people;
4. handle resistance to what you are doing in a respectful manner to turn people's views around;
5. embed your improved stakeholder engagement processes to enhance the way in which all of your projects and initiatives deliver change.

The Influence Agenda is strategic in scope

What *The Influence Agenda* can do that a single chapter of a project or change management text cannot is to look at stakeholder engagement as strategic activity. It places stakeholders at the heart of projects, change and, indeed, business as usual, recognising them as a vital part of creating successful change and running an effective business or operation. So, you will need a strategic approach to how you engage with groups and individuals, selecting which to prioritise and thinking about how you will develop relationships and build long-term engagement.

The Influence Agenda sees projects and change as a strategic tool for developing your organisation and propelling it towards a designed future. This makes stakeholders essential players in selecting and developing projects from the outset. Consequently, it places stakeholder engagement as a central role of an organisation rather than as a specific function of a few individuals within it. That is why *The Influence Agenda* ends with the biggest stakeholder agenda of all: considering how to go about creating a stakeholder engagement culture in your organisation and how to measure its maturity.

The stakeholder engagement process at the heart of *The Influence Agenda*

The Influence Agenda is arranged around a simple five-step process, which we will outline here and will give in more detail in Chapter 1.

1. Identify

Who are your stakeholders? And what are your strategic stakeholder engagement goals? By the end of Chapter 2, you will be able to answer these questions.

2. Analyse

The next step is to analyse your stakeholders to equip you to engage with them effectively. You also need to prioritise them so that you can focus your limited time and resources where they can have the greatest effect. And what resources do you have available? List the assets, skills, character, abilities and commitment of your team – and of yourself – and match these up to your stakeholder challenges. This will be a key factor in your success. By the end of Chapter 3, you will be able to assess your stakeholder landscape precisely and accurately.

3. Plan

Now it is time to build a structured yet flexible plan to achieve the strategic results you need. An essential component of your plan will be the messages you convey at each stage, along with your choice of media and the tone you want to strike. Communication is at the heart of stakeholder engagement. By the end of Chapter 4, you will be able to create compelling, persuasive and powerful messages and deliver them effectively. And, by the end of Chapter 8, you will be able to plan an engagement and communication campaign that will put you in control.

4. Act

Ultimately, you need to get out there and engage with your stakeholders… You have to listen, ask, persuade, cajole, tease, induce, counter, appease, collaborate and more.

As you do that, you will have successes and setbacks. Sometimes you will have to deal with resistance: resistance to your ideas, to your leadership and to the change you are trying to promote. By the end of Chapters 5, 6 and 7, you will be able to speak and argue persuasively, and handle resistance confidently.

5. Review

Sustainable success comes about through perseverance. You will need to monitor what you are doing and evaluate the results you are achieving (or not). This knowledge must lead to revised plans. By the end of Chapter 9, you will be able to keep on top of the constantly changing engagement environment and, as a bonus, you will also be able to start the conversations about changing the stakeholder engagement culture of your organisation.

What you get with *The Influence Agenda*

The Influence Agenda is not a 'how to' book, spelling out one sequence of actions to follow – stakeholder engagement is far more complicated than that. It does offer a master process, which works. But, more than anything else, it is a source book; a toolkit of resources for people who need to engage with stakeholders, influence their choices and manage the process. Consequently, you don't just get nine chapters of ideas, techniques and practical tools, you also get a whole array of resources:

- 10 appendices;
- 63 figures created for this book;
- 8 tables;
- 15 templates – all of which (and more) can be downloaded from *The Influence Agenda* website at www.theinfluenceagenda.co.uk.

Getting started with *The Influence Agenda*

As with all good books, Chapter 1 is where *The Influence Agenda* starts. In this chapter will answer five essential questions:

1. What … is *The Influence Agenda*?
2. Why in principle … the benefits of *The Influence Agenda*.
3. Why in practice … the evolution of power in organisations.
4. How in principle … the stakeholder engagement process.
5. How in practice … a roadmap through *The Influence Agenda*.

But before you get on to that, I invite you to read a short preliminary chapter, 'The Origin of Stakeholders'. It is only a short chapter and it is partly for fun – well, I enjoyed researching it – but I think you will learn something new and interesting. And it will introduce the first of my ten Stakeholder Rules.

The Origin of Stakeholders

The meaning of 'stakeholder'

In this book, we will use as simple a definition of the term 'stakeholder' as possible:

> **DEFINITION**
>
> *Stakeholder*: anyone who has any interest in what you are doing.

A stakeholder can be an individual or a group, with the word 'anyone' inviting us to draw our net as widely as possible. And any interest means that they can be interested in what you are doing, how you are doing it or its outcome.

A humorous alternative to this definition, which is equally wide and equally true, is that a stakeholder is 'anyone who can ruin your day'.

This word 'stakeholder' has, in the author's professional life, moved from being a jargon word that has been little understood outside narrow areas of business to becoming commonplace. So where does it come from?

The origin of stakeholders

According to *The Oxford English Dictionary* (2nd edn, 1991), the word 'stakeholder' first appeared in 1708, meaning the holder of a wager. A stake is 'that which is placed at hazard', although the *OED* is uncertain where that usage of stake comes from.

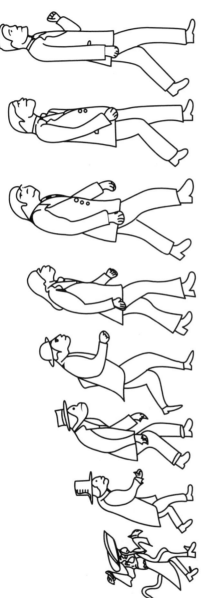

Early 18th century
Stakeholding exclusively part of gambling culture

Late 19th century
Primacy of the shareholder

1940s
Managers as trustees, balancing multiple communities

Early 1960s
'Stakeholder' identified as a concept

Late 1960s
Ansoff incorporates stakeholding into corporate strategy

Early 1980s
Freeman writes *Strategic Management: A Stakeholder Approach*

Mid-1990s
Tony Blair describes a stakeholder economy

2010s
Stakeholder Engagement starts to emerge as a managerial and professional discipline

FIGURE 0.1 The origin of stakeholders

The *OED* credits the first use of stakeholder in the business sense that interests us to Igor Ansoff in 1965, but my research shows a slightly different story.

Where to begin…

This is a practical rather than scholarly volume, but it does seem like a nice idea to trace the origins of the concept of stakeholders. After all, as we mean it, the word is a twentieth-century one, coined within the lifetime of the author. Yet etymology is a specialist discipline and even a recent coinage is hard to trace with authority. So what I offer you is a sketch of the history of a word whose fiftieth birthday – like that of this author – likely falls around the time of writing.

E. Merrick Dodd wrote an article in the *Harvard Law Review* (Volume 45: 1145–63) in May 1932 entitled 'For Whom are Corporate Managers Trustees?' and entered into a debate about the proper purpose of the corporation and the roles of its managers. He argued that these included creating secure jobs for employees, making better-quality products for customers and contributing to the welfare of the community. We can now see this as a very modern agenda in favour of stakeholders. Dodd was arguing against an article that appeared in the same journal a year earlier by A.A. Berle, who argued for the primacy of shareholders as the owners of the business.

Dodd's view was very much endorsed by oil executive Frank W. Abrams in a *Harvard Business Review* article entitled 'Management's Responsibilities in a Complex World' and published in May 1951. In this, he too sought to balance the interests of stockholders against those of employees, customers and the public.

Yet, just seven years later, in 1958, Milton Friedman – as we might expect of a free-market libertarian – challenged this view head-on:

> If anything is certain to destroy our free society, to undermine its very foundations, it would be a widespread acceptance by management of social responsibilities in some sense other than to make as much money as possible. This is a fundamentally subversive doctrine.

Friedman's view did not prevail, for all of the political influence it was to have in the UK and US in the 1980s.

The term 'stakeholder' is adopted

With the idea of stakeholders very much in the air, a word was needed, and the term 'stakeholder' was first coined at the Stanford Research Institute in 1963 as a play on the words 'shareholder' and 'stockholder'.

It was shortly afterwards that Igor Ansoff briefly discussed stakeholder theory in his 1965 book *Corporate Strategy*. He argued, like Dodd and Abrams, that companies had responsibilities to various stakeholders, including workers, suppliers, managers and, of course, stockholders. Each constituency must get some satisfaction from the actions of the corporation.

Stakeholder theory took off as a discipline in 1983 when R. Edward Freeman wrote *Strategic Management: A Stakeholder Approach*. This is widely seen as a classic business book, focusing on business ethics in the widest sense, and influenced a whole field of study that has followed it.

From then on, the term became widely used, especially by politicians and social planners. Its usage in the political domain reached its zenith in the UK when Prime Minister Tony Blair floated the concept of a 'stakeholder economy' in a speech in January 1996, fully reversing the Thatcherite/Friedman rejection of society and replacing it with the idea that all of us are stakeholders in our society.

Usage in project and change management

Throughout the late 1980s and early 1990s, the word 'stakeholder' was becoming more and more widely used. It was now that the term started to become a part of the jargon of project management and the management of change in organisational settings.

This was a move away from the central idea of stakeholder theory that organisations have a responsibility to meet the needs of stakeholders. It moved towards a pragmatic recognition that, in making changes, organisations must balance the diverse needs and agendas of different stakeholders, and manage the impact of their responses to change.

Stakeholders have an interest in what we are doing and how we are doing it. They are affected by the process or the outcome and they can often have an impact on what we are doing. Consequently, project managers increasingly realised that the success of their projects and change initiatives was intimately dependent upon stakeholders.

And so we get to Stakeholder Rule Number 1: *your stakeholders will determine the success, or not, of your project.*

The strongest single example on this happened a year before Tony Blair's speech mentioned above, with some things that happened in 1995. These events accelerated the profile of stakeholders among project managers and led to a 130-page dossier about how things can all go horribly wrong for a company that neglects some of its stakeholders. So, it is time to read Chapter 1 and find out what happened.

chapter **1**

The Process is Trivial: The Implementation is Not

In December 1994, the UK Government gave approval for the deep water disposal of a redundant oil storage platform owned by Shell and Esso, and operated by Shell. That platform was Brent Spar.

Shell, which had responsibility for the decommissioning, approached the project carefully. It reviewed options, carried out impact assessments, commissioned reports, consulted and finally sought formal approval from regulators and from the UK Government.

Brent Spar was big: 137 metres tall and displacing 66,000 tonnes. The plan was to tow it into deep water in the North Atlantic and use shaped explosives to sink it. Analysis suggested damage to the deep sea marine environment would be minimal.

In February 1995, however, the environmental campaigning organisation Greenpeace learned of the plan and organised a worldwide campaign. In support of this, 23 activists and journalists occupied Brent Spar. Their campaign led to widespread boycotts of Shell service stations and rapidly growing damage to Shell's international reputation.

The end result was that Shell felt compelled to reverse its decision and radically alter its plans for disposal. It put the eventual cost of disposal at £60 million, but this fails to account for loss of business and reputational damage. In an article for the magazine *Greenpeace Business* in April 2005,

James Smith, the Country Chairman of Shell UK, referred to the public outrage, writing:

> We had learned that, while good science and regulatory approval are essential, they are not sufficient. We needed to engage with society – understanding and responding to people's concerns and expectations. We had to be clearer and more transparent about our plans and actions.

What is the Influence Agenda?

Put simply, the Influence Agenda is the process of engaging fully with all of your stakeholders. As the Brent Spar case illustrates, the Influence Agenda must dominate your thinking, your planning and your actions whenever you seek to make important changes in your organisation. This is the reason why Stakeholder Rule Number 2 is true: *projects and change would be easy if it were not for the people involved.*

FIGURE 1.1 **Stakeholder model**

Your stakeholders

If your success depends on the positive participation, endorsement or, at the very least, support of your stakeholders, we need to understand who they are. At its simplest, a stakeholder model needs to account for ten constituencies.

Each party to this model has its own agenda: its own wants, needs, perceptions and prejudices. And often these compete, leading to friction and conflict, not just with your organisation or project, but with one another. This means that, often, satisfying one stakeholder can alienate another, as you seek to address different personalities, clashes of goals and competition for influence.

Stakeholder management?

We frequently hear the term 'stakeholder management'. However, managing relationships with and between diverse people and groups is unlikely to ever succeed. Indeed, the attempt itself may be perceived as disrespectful and manipulative. At best, stakeholder management is little more than a tick-list approach to scheduled communication – often more focused on giving to than on receiving from stakeholders. The Brent Spar case showed us that this cannot work.

What makes far more sense is to engage with stakeholders to build collaborative relationships at the right level. This requires an integrated approach that takes full account of all of your stakeholders and how they inter-relate with one another. This is a long-term strategy that begins at the very start of your project and will often persist beyond its formal completion and handover.

Stakeholder engagement

Giving up the certainty of developing the solution, deciding what to do, doing it and then, if necessary, defending it is hard. The poverty of this 'Four-D' approach, however, is clear from the Brent Spar example given above and the alternative 'Three-D' approach is, in the end, often quicker as well as more certain: dialogue, decide and do. Your investment in dialogue at the outset will obviate the need to defend and then, frequently, start again.

FIGURE 1.2 ╱ Five things to understand deeply

Engaging openly and respectfully with stakeholders is a genuine act of leadership: it empowers others to participate in a process and to feel a genuine commitment to its outcomes. This can only enhance your own leadership status and effectiveness, as well as strengthen the delivery of change to your organisation.

Effective engagement requires a depth of understanding of five things:

1. People and how the relationships between them work.
2. Organisations and how power and influence work within them.
3. The context within which you are operating and its political, social, commercial, technological, economic, environmental and regulatory constraints.
4. The situation you want to change and the implications that this change will have.
5. The tools and process of influence, and how to apply them effectively.

╱ The benefits of the Influence Agenda

Setting aside the time and resources needed to engage actively with a wide range of stakeholders is a big undertaking, so you need to be confident that the investment is worthwhile. There are two directions from which to develop your business case for engagement, asking:

1. what if we do engage fully with stakeholders (the positive benefits and the costs of engagement)?
2. what if we don't engage fully with stakeholders (the savings and the adverse risks of not engaging)?

Whilst quantifying these is not going to be straightforward, you might like to start by estimating the value of engagement under the headings of benefits and risks that can be averted.

Table 1.1   The benefits of the Influence Agenda

Positive Benefits of Stakeholder Engagement	Risks that Can Be Averted by Stakeholder Engagement
❏ Raised levels and accuracy of stakeholder awareness ❏ Promoting essential messages and ideas ❏ Increase in stakeholder commitment ❏ Value of improved solutions leading to enhanced likelihood and degree of success ❏ Reduction in the range and intensity of resistance ❏ Shortening of implementation phase and reduction of budget ❏ Reputational enhancement at organisational and personal levels ❏ Personal development and job satisfaction ❏ Improved long-term personal, professional and organisational relationships	❏ Reputational risks ❏ Delay ❏ Cancellation or failure ❏ Additional costs ❏ Mismatch between required and actual specification ❏ Missing an enhanced solution ❏ Benefits not being fully realised ❏ Non-cooperation or even sabotage ❏ Legitimate concerns not being voiced ❏ Industrial action ❏ Legal or regulatory infringement ❏ Outcomes not being accepted by stakeholders

How does *The Influence Agenda* differ from other influence or persuasion books?

There are a lot of books on the market (including one of my own: *Brilliant Influence*) on the general topics of influence and persuasion. Each offers ways to influence individuals, using approaches as diverse as plain common sense at one extreme, such as Dale Carnegie's evergreen *How to Win Friends and Influence People*, via Robert Cialdini's business psychology classic *Influence: The Science and Practice* to the other extreme of surprising insights from more recent (2010) advanced research, such as Kevin Dutton's popular analysis of split-second persuasion, *Flipnosis*.

The Influence Agenda is not just about influencing an individual – it is about how to plan and execute a campaign to engage with and influence a wide variety of different individuals and groups. Along the way, you will learn how to identify who to engage with, and how to assess each stakeholder and how prioritise your efforts. You will learn the different strategies to apply and a wide variety of tactics that will work. And we will consider stakeholder engagement in a wide range of contexts.

These contexts are set out in Appendix 1, which lists 45 typical scenarios under eight headings:

- Business projects
- Business transformation
- Process change
- Cultural transformation
- Cyclical change
- Community projects
- Governmental projects
- Crises

The strategic scope of 'the Influence Agenda'

It is very easy to quickly get caught up in tactical, day-to-day stakeholder communication, focusing your attention on responding to immediate problems or, at best, on planning how to take the next step. These tactical skills are important, but *The Influence Agenda* also offers a strategic context, which sets a direction and purpose for your stakeholder engagement.

Think of strategy as a compass bearing, selecting where you want to go and why. We start our strategic journey by thinking about our reasons for, and the outcome we want to generate from, engaging. This leads us to set out what results, or outputs, we need to achieve. Only from here can we start to plan how we will achieve them.

As such, this book is strategic in its scope:

- It places stakeholder engagement at the heart of projects, change and, indeed, 'business as usual' activities, recognising that stakeholders

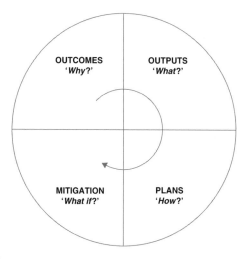

FIGURE 1.3 / Strategy development and deployment cycle

are a vital part of creating successful change and running an effective business or operation.

- It sees projects and change themselves as strategic tools for developing your organisation and propelling it towards a designed future. Consequently, stakeholders need to be active participants in selecting and developing projects from the outset.
- It places stakeholder engagement as a core role of an organisation rather than as a specific function of a few individuals within it. Indeed, in Chapter 9, we will consider how to go about creating a stakeholder engagement culture in your organisation and how to measure its maturity.
- Finally, it takes a strategic approach to the way we engage with groups and individuals, selecting which to prioritise and creating strategies for long-term engagement and relationship development.

The evolution of power in organisations

There was a time when organisations would not have contemplated engaging with stakeholders. In the command and control corporations of the nineteenth century, everything was subordinate to the desires of the owners, who exerted a high degree of 'coercive power' over labour. To the extent that these organisations considered their wider communities, it was usually out of self-interest or, at best, a paternalistic sense of obligation.

There were exceptions, however. Many Quaker-run businesses in the UK, like Cadbury, took a socially oriented approach to providing amenities for their staff and the communities around them. They recognised that, by instilling the right values, they could access greater levels of loyalty – and therefore performance – than a coercive approach could achieve.

Today, there remain a few businesses and organisations which primarily wield what Amitai Etzioni called 'normative power'; securing compliance through shared beliefs and values. Most of those that do are in the voluntary, campaigning and caring sectors, although there are some in the commercial sector too. In the UK, these include the Co-operative Society and the John Lewis Partnership. Most businesses and public sector organisations prefer what Etzioni termed 'utilitarian power'. Put simply, they exchange rewards for compliance, establishing a trading relationship with their employees.

Etzioni's three forms of organisational power are reflected in three principal approaches to stakeholders – compulsion, reciprocation and genuine engagement – which he described in his 1961 book *A Comparative Analysis of Complex Organizations: On Power, Involvement, and their Correlates*. There is a role for each of these, but here we shall focus on engagement.

Fragmentation and complexity

Another important feature of power in organisations is its fragmentation across many dimensions. In a typical large corporation, government department, public authority or charity, power is divided among many departments and often across different geographical elements. Indeed, many corporations are now made up of individual trading businesses, each vying with one another for power. In some, the competition between them is an unfortunate consequence of human nature; in others, it is deliberately engineered by senior executives.

This fragmentation results in a highly tactical approach to stakeholders as different parts of the organisation prioritise different stakeholders and even send conflicting messages. Take, for example: the customers, whom the sales team might prioritise; the staff, whom the personnel function will favour; the media, on whom the public affairs focus; and the suppliers, with whom the purchasing team work. Whilst there is a genuine community of interest among them, the organisation must take a strategic view to ensure that it emphasises these common themes.

Increasingly, therefore, we hear of organisations described as complex systems of interacting and interdependent agents. The role of the organisation is to find and exploit opportunities so the whole system can benefit. The system metaphor is seductive and no doubt highly valuable, but its very complexity makes it somewhat intractable to the average manager or change leader.

A profitable starting place is to borrow from Six Sigma, a structured methodology to drive process improvement developed in the 1980s by Motorola. An important concept in Six Sigma is that of Xs and Ys. A Y is a measure of output performance. It is an effect of the process. Motorola talked of Big Ys as the things that matter most to the business' most critical customers. An X is a cause – a factor, variable or process element which can affect the outcome. The Big Xs are the factors that have the greatest impact on the Big Ys.

The way we simplify the complexity of a highly interconnected system of stakeholders is to look for the Big Ys and then for the Big Xs. In our case, the Big Ys represent the important changes we want to create: the outcomes. The Big Xs are the stakeholders who can have the maximum impact upon those outcomes.

This is the approach we will take in *The Influence Agenda*, so let us look at the overall process that we will use.

The stakeholder engagement process

If you want to make change happen in your organisation, if you are responsible for a programme of activities or for a single project, or if you are pursuing a new initiative within your department, you will need to engage with your stakeholders and manage the consequences of their actions.

Engaging stakeholders is at the heart of all project and change management. Like risk management, it is not a simple bolt-on activity, but needs to be integral to the design of your project, to your planning processes and to your daily management activities.

Without sufficient stakeholder support, your project and the changes it is designed to bring about will fail. Happily, the stakeholder engagement process is, fundamentally, simple. It has five steps, each with two principal components.

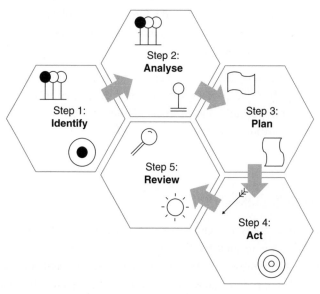

FIGURE 1.4 / The stakeholder engagement process

Step 1: identify

The first step is to identify who your stakeholders are: individuals and groups. To do this, the simplest and often best approach is to gather a diverse group of colleagues and get each one to suggest anyone they can think of who might have any interest in your project. Create and continue to grow your list throughout the project.

It is during this step that you also need to identify your strategic stakeholder engagement goals with regard to your project: what do you need to achieve to maximise the chances of your project succeeding? You will do this in the context of your organisation's purpose and goals, and those of your project or change programme.

This step is the subject of Chapter 2.

Step 2: analyse

Once you have identified who your stakeholders are, the next step is to analyse them. The more you understand about them, the better equipped you will be to engage with them effectively. You also need to prioritise your stakeholders so that you and your team can focus your limited time and resources where they will have most effect.

It is during this step too that you will need to list the resources and team you have available: the assets, skills, character, abilities and commitment of your team – and of yourself. Matching these up to your stakeholder challenges effectively will be a key factor in your success.

This step is the subject of Chapter 3.

Step 3: plan

Once you understand your stakeholders and resources, it is time to build a plan. Avoid the temptation to dive into engagement. Instead, create a structured yet flexible sequence of actions that are designed to achieve the strategic results you need. The broad thrust of your plan will arise naturally from your analysis, but each situation and stakeholder is different, and your plan needs to be tailored to the detail of the particular circumstances at hand.

An essential component of your plan is to devise the messages you will convey at each stage, along with your choice of media and the tone you want to strike. Communication is at the heart of stakeholder engagement.

This step is the subject of Chapters 4 and 8.

Step 4: act

And then you have to get out there and engage with your stakeholders... You have to listen, ask, persuade, cajole, tease, induce, counter, appease, collaborate and more.

And as you do that, you will have successes and setbacks. Sometimes you will have to deal with resistance; resistance to your ideas, to your leadership and to the change you are trying to promote. Handling resistance is one of the biggest challenges on your Influence Agenda.

This step is the subject of Chapters 5, 6 and 7.

Step 5: review

The process so far is guaranteed to work ... sometimes. Real, sustainable success comes about through perseverance. You need to monitor what you are doing and constantly evaluate the results you are achieving (or not), and feed that new knowledge into revised plans.

Day by day and even hour by hour, you will be making changes to your approach to adapt it to the new prevailing conditions, to the changes in your stakeholders' perceptions and to new events. The monitor and control loop at the heart of the review step is the secret to success: the more rapidly you cycle around that loop, the sooner you will pick up small but important details and address them. If you cycle around the loop too slowly, small problems will escalate rapidly and will be large ones before you become aware of them. The monitor and control loop is your means of controlling your project and of staying in control of your engagement process.

This step is the subject of Chapter 9.

Simple is not easy

The five-step process given above is simple – but simple is not the same as easy. Following these steps relentlessly, remaining objective and keeping consistent, day after day, in the face of complex, demanding and sometimes uncomfortable project challenges is hard.

And that is not all. The other big factor in making stakeholder engagement difficult is the 'knowing-doing gap'. It is simple to read a book like this, understand it and then think you can go out and do it well. The reality, of course, is quite different. Good stakeholder engagement is a craft – a set of skills and attitudes that you will develop over a lifetime of practising and developing. A good metaphor here is the traditional three-stage model of progression within any of the trades. This is a model that goes back to medieval times, when a young person (a boy in those days) entered their chosen trade as an apprentice. They trained and worked for many years to acquire the skills and knowledge to work unsupervised as a journeyman. After many years perfecting their craft, they would finally be recognised as a master, becoming able to work to the highest standards on the most demanding jobs and, as a result, being ready to take on and supervise their own apprentice.

This book is written for apprentices and journeymen. It will give an apprentice all that they need to understand the basics of their stakeholder engagement craft. And it will give the journeyman new ideas to help them on their journey to perfect their craft. But no master ever considers their journey over. They will always be stretching themselves and taking on new challenges to develop their craft. I hope one or two masters will find some insights in this book to help them develop their craft too.

WISE WORDS FROM REAL PRACTITIONERS

Your emotion about an event dictates the results you will get. Controlling your emotions is essential if you are going to manage your stakeholders well and vital if you are to retain control of events.

A roadmap through *The Influence Agenda*

Now we have introduced the stakeholder engagement process that we will use throughout this book, let's review the route through the next nine chapters.

Chapter 2: Who are Your Stakeholders?

We will start by thinking about the strategic context and what you want to achieve, and will then turn our attention to the practical ways you and your team can identify who your stakeholders are. This chapter will also introduce the principal tool for structured stakeholder engagement: the stakeholder register.

Chapter 3: More than Just Power: Analysing Your Stakeholders

Stakeholder power is important, but so are other characteristics. We will consider the stakeholder analysis process in two stages: a quick and simple triage to discern the most salient features; and then a more in-depth analysis of your stakeholders and the relationships among them. This chapter is a powerhouse of practical tools and techniques that will extend you kit bag, even if you are a seasoned practitioner. It closes with the crucial analysis of you and your team – the resources, skills and experience you can bring to bear when you engage with your stakeholders.

Chapter 4: What are You Doing? Crafting Your Message

This chapter is all about communication: the basics, how to plan your engagement process and how to craft your message to make it compelling, persuasive and powerful. This is supplemented by two further chapters about the craft of persuasion.

Chapter 5: Gentle Persuasion: Soft Power

Gentle persuasion is about the classic craft of influencing people to accept your point of view. It will take you through all of the basics of influence and what makes people influential, and then offers a range of techniques for deploying your influence, before ratcheting up the pressure to gentle persuasion, finishing with negotiation as a gentle approach to conflict.

Chapter 6: Hidden Persuasion: Behavioural Economics

One of the biggest and most rapidly growing areas of interest to policy-makers and business professionals since the start of the twenty-first century has been the emerging science of 'behavioural economics'. This departs from traditional economic theory in recognising that human behaviour is far from rational, yet is statistically predictable if we can gather enough data and characterise the situation sharply enough. Behavioural economics is increasingly offering us more and better tools to help our stakeholders make the right decisions. But how it is used is a matter of some debate, which will take us into a discussion of the ethics of stakeholder engagement.

Chapter 7: A Dozen Reasons Why You're Wrong: Handling Resistance

Resistance is an inevitable response to change, yet it is one of the most feared aspects of change among project and change leaders. So this chapter sets out to demonstrate how you can understand and engage positively with resistance. It uses a simple onion model of resistance, developed by the author, and applies this to a range of specific resistance problems, culminating in the ultimate form of resistance: conflict.

Chapter 8: Your Influence Agenda: Campaign Planning

The Influence Agenda is about a strategic approach to stakeholder engagement, so this chapter provides you with the tools to build a strategic campaign, to coordinate your team and to work with the media. The media forms an important part of your campaign, playing two roles: as stakeholders and as a medium with which to communicate with your stakeholders.

Chapter 9: Making it Work: Campaign Management

The monitor and control loop is the beating heart of a successful stake-holder engagement campaign. This chapter goes further by also looking at how to evaluate your campaign, how to learn from it and how to build a positive stakeholder engagement culture within your organisation.

A Call to Action

Of course, we end the book with a few words by way of summary, but essentially with some thoughts to wish you well.

WISE WORDS FROM REAL PRACTITIONERS

It can sometimes be surprising just how little time and effort it really takes to get results. A short phone call can have a big impact on your influence. People are nearly always receptive to a personal call, so use this personal touch to your advantage.

chapter 2

Who are Your Stakeholders?

The story of the Anglo-French supersonic airliner Concorde is one of high technology and stakeholders. Without a doubt, the technology was exceptional: its only competitor as a commercial supersonic passenger plane, the Soviet Tupolev Tu-144, which flew only 55 scheduled passenger flights before safety concerns caused the operator to use it solely for cargo.

Concorde was the result of political decisions in France and the UK to collaborate, motivated partly by the high commercial cost of development and partly by the desire to improve political harmony and agreement. The naming clearly reflected that and, out of a spirit of concord, the British even chose to adopt the French spelling.

So, it was Concorde until the UK Prime Minister, Harold Macmillan, perceived some minor disrespect from the French President, Charles de Gaulle, and changed the UK name of the plane to Concord, the British spelling. This was later reversed again by Tony Benn, a minister in a later government, to mark the first public appearance of the plane in France in 1967, declaring that the extra 'e' stood for 'Excellence, England, Europe and Entente [Cordiale]'. A Scots correspondent complained that he spoke of '"E" for England, but part of it is made in Scotland', to which Benn masterfully replied that it was also '"E" for "Écosse" [the French name for Scotland]'.

So far, the story of Concorde appears to be one of largely successful political stakeholder engagement. Certainly its construction was a huge technical success. So why was Concorde a commercial failure, with planes being sold only to two airlines: the largest in Britain and France? The answer is largely in the failure to consider a set of vital stakeholders: the countries over whose airspace Concorde would need to fly. Fears about the impact of the sonic boom that the plane made in supersonic flight meant that many countries, such as India, forbade supersonic flight through their airspace. This resulted in too few international routes being available for supersonic flight.

Some have gone further and have argued, with merit, that the principal stakeholder engagement problem was the failure to secure long-haul routes over mainland USA, closing off many lucrative markets. It is quite possible that much US opposition flowed from a 'not invented here' attitude to the plane, given that two competing US designs were abandoned in 1971.

Ultimately, failure to properly engage with the USA may have denied the plane access to the routes which could have made it a profitable aircraft for many airlines. If one of the big US aircraft manufacturers had been invited to collaborate with the British and the French, the story might have been different, but the problem started when Concorde became primarily a political venture.

What do you want to achieve?

Concorde was, ultimately, a commercial venture that needed access to commercially important long-haul routes. Knowing what you want – and need – to achieve is the vital context for stakeholder identification. So start by asking yourself: 'What is our purpose in engaging with stakeholders?'

The answer to this question creates your stakeholder engagement goal, which needs to be aligned with the deeper goals of the project, programme or change you are working to deliver. These, in turn, will align with your organisation's purpose – or mission as it is often called.

Organisational Goal
Purpose, mission, values

Programme, Project or Change Goal
What you are trying to achieve

Stakeholder Engagement Goal
What you need to achieve to maximise chances of project or change programme success

FIGURE 2.1   Stakeholder engagement goal

In thinking about your organisation's purpose, you may want to be mindful of its wider responsibilities beyond financial profit. This will come naturally to organisations in the public and third sectors, and is increasingly central to the thinking of a wide range of commercial organisations.

INFLUENTIAL IDEA: THE TRIPLE BOTTOM LINE

The idea of a triple bottom line was coined by John Elkington, founder of the UK consultancy SustainAbility, in 1994, shortly before Tony Blair coined the term 'stakeholder economy'. He suggested that, in addition to the usual profit-based bottom line measure of a company's performance, businesses should also prepare bottom line measures in a 'people account' and a 'planet account', giving rise to the three pillars of profit, people and planet.

These are often represented as three overlapping circles of concern that clearly represent three views of overlapping stakeholder groups:

- 'Profit' represents the economic imperative felt by owners and shareholders, whose concern is for monetary reward and the growth of capital.

- 'People' represents the needs of the organisation's community and therefore its corporate social responsibilities.

- 'Planet' represents the natural environment and the part that an organisation must play in our joint responsibility for its stewardship.

Elkington describes the triple bottom line in his 1997 book *Cannibals with Forks: The Triple Bottom Line of 21st Century Business*.

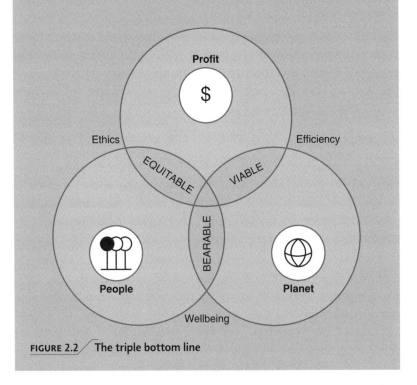

FIGURE 2.2 The triple bottom line

Wise goals

The goals you set need to be both smart (specific, meaningful, achievable, responsible and time-bound) and also wise.

Difference

For a goal to be wise, it must make a difference that matters – a valuable contribution to your chances of sustainable success.

Unintended consequences

Goals create change, which can have unintended consequences. You must carefully evaluate the possible consequences of working towards your goals and of achieving them. You cannot eliminate the truly unknowable, but you can invest the effort needed to turn as much as possible of the unknown risk into known risk to create a strong basis for evaluating your choices.

Measured risk

You must also assess how much risk is appropriate in the context of your project, compare this with the level of risk of your chosen stakeholder engagement goals and then consider whether the two are consistent. If you will not bear the whole impact of any unfavourable consequence, what about the people who will?

Bystanders and participants

A range of stakeholders will be involved in your efforts to create change. How will your choices affect them? Your actions will be motivated primarily by your own reasons, yet it is possible to make choices that include a measure of generosity towards others, to mitigate the consequences for stakeholders who are directly affected.

Staying alert for change

Goals engender a sense of focus. You can soon find yourself more on a railway track than on a flight path. Seeing few alternatives, it is easy to get into an 'I've started so I will finish' mindset. But if your goals are worthwhile, they may also take time to deliver. What if things change along the way? What if you change? What if new experiences and opportunities come along? A wise goal is one that allows for modification, change or replacement. Stay open to outside influences.

Evidence procedure

Knowing when you have achieved your goal, so that you know when to stop pursuing it, is critical. Develop an objective measure by which you will know you have succeeded. This 'how will you know when you've got it?' test is your evidence procedure and will enable you to invest the right amount of resources in your stakeholder engagement.

The influencer–sponsor relationship

In considering your goals, they must be fully aligned between you and your sponsor. The sponsor is the senior person who takes overall responsibility for the change you are engaged in promoting. They will often be the conspicuous senior advocate for the change and will usually have a measure of decision-making and oversight authority.

The sponsor's role in stakeholder engagement is critical and not simply because of their advocacy role and the part they play in promoting the change. The example they set in either supporting or undermining your campaign will affect how others interpret your messages.

There are three scenarios, which we can call trapezoidal, square and triangular relationships.

The trapezoidal relationship

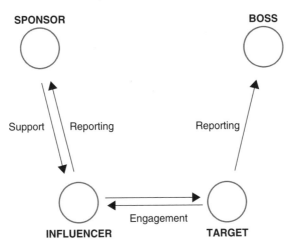

FIGURE 2.3 The trapezoidal relationship

The simplest case is where the sponsor has no relationship with the people to whom the target of your stakeholder engagement reports. The sponsor therefore has no mechanism to influence your target indirectly and their role must be to support you as influencer.

The square relationship

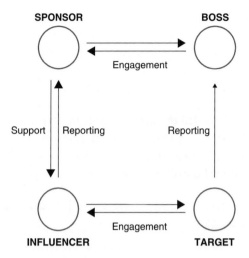

FIGURE 2.4 The square relationship

Where your sponsor has a relationship with the boss of your engagement target, their high-level influence must reinforce yours or will risk undermining it. A sponsor who does not actively 'sponsor' their project will not be seen as committed to that project, and others will wonder why they, in turn, should be.

The triangular relationship

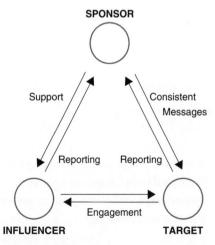

FIGURE 2.5   The triangular relationship

Your target may report directly to your sponsor, in which case you would expect that the messages your sponsor gives them will mesh completely with the messages you are giving. They may choose for you to be the principal influencer, but if there is any sense that your message conflicts with theirs, the stakeholder will immediately discount yours and, worse, may try to play you and your sponsor off against each other.

Methods for stakeholder identification

The tried-and-trusted way of identifying stakeholders is to gather together a number of people and ask them all to contribute their ideas in some form of brainstorming session. This works, but only up to a point. The risks are that large groups become focused on the ideas of a few individuals, generating variants on a theme, or that quieter individuals find it hard to be heard. Without a doubt, more heads means more ideas, but how can you optimise the process?

Brainwriting

Brainwriting is an excellent facilitation method which overcomes the shortcomings of the more familiar brainstorming. It certainly removes the risk of some people's voices carrying more weight due to personality or perceptions, and it can also readily move you into the analysis stage that we will examine in Chapter 3.

The process starts with selecting your participants. The best approach is to maximise the diversity of your group, selecting a range of people with different backgrounds, professional disciplines, experiences and perspectives. If your group is too homogeneous, then they will each give you many of the same ideas. Selecting for diversity optimises your chances of spotting 'outlier stakeholders' – those whom most people would fail to notice as having a stake.

Sit your group around a table, or around a number of tables, sharing a small empty basket, box or bucket between five or six people. Each of these subgroups should also have access to a large pile of blank index cards and everyone will need a pen or pencil.

Explain the project or change, answering any questions that arise, and then set out the task of identifying stakeholders, encouraging the widest possible interpretation of the term. Now give everybody ten minutes to think of as many as they can. Participants must write the name and description of each stakeholder or stakeholder group they identify on a new card and place it into the basket. After ten minutes, each basket will contain a whole wealth of cards.

Now give the group a second ten-minute burst. Have them take any card and record any further stakeholders that this card prompts in their mind on a new card. If you have multiple groups, you can repeat this step, swapping baskets around.

Now you have a set of cards with many stakeholders recorded. If you wanted to, you could use these for analysis, grouping the cards together in clusters (and eliminating duplicates). Another way to use the cards and the group to analyse your stakeholders is to give each subgroup a portion of the cards and set the groups an analysis task, such as scoring each card by power and noting down what that stakeholder's agenda is likely to be. In Chapter 3, we will examine a whole array of factors you can use to analyse your stakeholders.

Stakeholder lists

Another good way to create a list of stakeholders is to modify a pre-existing list. You may have stakeholder lists prepared for other projects and you will certainly be able to trawl published organisational documents like annual reports, strategy documents and business plans for stakeholders.

If you do not have a list, you might like to use the sample list in Appendix 2 as a stimulus for creating your own.

Scenarios and storytelling

An informal way of identifying stakeholders is to create scenarios of how your project will play out through the planning, delivery, integration and operational stages by using a storytelling approach. As you go through your story, stop at each project stage and ask questions like the following:

1. Who is instrumental in making things happen?
2. Who should we be talking with?
3. Who is getting in the way?
4. Who is holding vital resources?
5. Who has useful skills or knowledge?
6. Who is benefiting?
7. Who is losing out?

8. Who has to make compromises because of what we are doing?
9. Who is getting kudos or credit – or claiming it?
10. Who is feeling criticised?

Have the majority of your group work together to create the story, with each person looking for added detail. One or two members of the group would be tasked with listening for characters (stakeholders) who are referenced, either directly or indirectly. They would then record them as they appear as stakeholders, along with relevant details that will be useful in the analysis stage.

Task-by-task assessment

If you want a formal way of identifying your project stakeholders, there is nothing more robust than working from your work breakdown structure. This is a detailed document showing all of the tasks within the project structured into groups with common themes. To identify stakeholders, you can ask the following questions of each task:

1. Who is involved in making this task happen?
2. Who will observe the task in progress?
3. Who will have an opinion about this task – and whose opinions matter?
4. Who has access to the resources needed for this task?
5. Who needs to know about this task?
6. Who can support or frustrate the progress of this task?
7. Who is affected when the task is being carried out?
8. Who will evaluate this task?
9. Who will complain if it goes wrong?
10. Who will be impacted by the outcome of this task?

Horizon scanning

Horizon scanning is a process of looking into the future to see what changes may emerge as pressures on your project. It offers us a way to foresee which stakeholders might take an interest in our project and who might be affected by it.

A neat acronym, SPECTRES, will give you a mnemonic for recalling eight sources of stakeholder interest:

Social   What social impacts will your project have?
What are the various communities that it will affect?

Political	What are the political pressures on your project?
	What political ramifications could it have?
Economic	Where is the funding coming from?
	Who will be affected economically by your project?
Commercial	What people and organisations are in your supply chain?
	Who will be commercially affected by your project?
Technological	Who will evaluate, supply, configure and maintain the technology?
	Who are the users who will need to adapt to the new technology?
Regulatory	What regulatory regimes are you subject to?
	Who will have an interest in what your regulators do and say?
Environmental	How might your project affect the environment?
	Who cares about your impact on the environment?
Security	Whose safety or security will be affected by your project?
	Who will have fears about their safety or security?

Staff questionnaires

Some of the techniques we have just looked at can be formalised into a staff questionnaire to gather ideas from a wide range of colleagues about which stakeholders you should be engaging. As with the brainwriting process, you can use the questionnaire to go beyond a list and access people's perceptions of the priority you should be giving to each stakeholder, their evaluation of the potential impact and interests of the stakeholders, and the benefits of engaging with them. You may even be able to gain some ideas as to how to engage them and productive strategies to win them over.

Finally, engaging directly with colleagues – whether through a questionnaire, interviews, focus groups or simple conversations – is itself a form of stakeholder engagement. It is also a powerful way to build allies and look for volunteers in helping you to engage with other stakeholders.

The stakeholder register

If you are serious about tracking your stakeholders, analysing them and recording your conclusions, planning your campaign and tracking your progress, then one of your most valuable tools will be the stakeholder register. This is a formal record of all of your stakeholders and all of your analysis and engagement activities.

The sections that the stakeholder register will contain will be as follows:

- Section 1: identification information
- Section 2: stakeholder analysis
- Section 3: stakeholder engagement plan
- Section 4: stakeholder engagement monitoring

Section 1: identification information (supported by Chapter 2)

This section will contain a name and descriptor for your stakeholder or stakeholder group, along with useful biographical details. Typically these will include organisational affiliation, role or job title and contact details.

An important tip here is do not include more information than is useful. Ask yourself: if we include this information, how will it help us? If it will not, gathering and recording it will be a waste of your time.

Section 2: stakeholder analysis (supported by Chapter 3)

When you have determined what aspects of your stakeholder analysis (see Chapter 3) are relevant to understanding stakeholders and planning constructive engagement, record these in section 2 of your stakeholder register. This will include things like their influence or power, their interest in and attitude to the project, and who they are connected to. You may also classify the stakeholder so that you can easily extract a subset of stakeholders from your register. The list in Appendix 2 is divided into a simple classification scheme. Stakeholder analysis is the subject of Chapter 3.

Section 3: stakeholder engagement plan (supported by Chapter 8)

In this section, record your objectives with respect to each stakeholder and the actions you plan to take to achieve them. This section may become your principal management tool and we shall examine it in more detail in Chapter 8.

Section 4: stakeholder engagement monitoring (supported by Chapter 9)

As you progress with your plan, use this section to track and review progress, revisiting it from time to time. This section of the process is detailed in Chapter 9.

You can download a sample stakeholder register spreadsheet template from www.theinfluenceagenda.co.uk.

Database tools

For large, long-term programmes, you ought to consider building a full database solution that will allow you to tag stakeholders with many of the characteristics that interest you so that you can extract information and management reports. One benefit of this is that, with a simple web-based front end, you can gather data via questionnaires and self-reporting by stakeholders with little effort. The challenge of automation is in validating the quality of the data you gather.

This can be a substantial task and the partial solution is to develop a well-structured spreadsheet.

CRM software

The other alternative to building a database is to buy something off the shelf and many commercial customer relationship management (CRM) systems can readily be adapted to manage stakeholder engagement.

Big enterprise-level CRM solutions often offer this sort of functionality (Oracle and SAP are examples) with configurable functions that go beyond recording stakeholders as database entries by also offering configurable reports to stakeholders and even automated outbound stakeholder communication functions.

At the other end of the scale, there are numerous cloud-based CRM applications that you could consider adapting to your needs. Think in advance about the functionality you consider to be necessary, ideal, desirable and unwanted – your musts, should, coulds and won'ts – sometimes referred to as 'MoSCoW analysis'. Then evaluate around half-a-dozen CRM applications against your list of criteria. Aside from functional needs, also consider:

- ease of use;
- accessibility to your team members;
- pricing and volumes;
- uptime and service support arrangements;
- data security (from loss and from unauthorised access) and back-up of your information should the provider cease trading.

WISE WORDS FROM REAL PRACTITIONERS: CROSS-CULTURAL STAKEHOLDER ENGAGEMENT

The vast majority of second-language speakers are constantly translating what they hear inside their head. Only people with deep immersion hear a foreign language and process it instantly. So when speaking with non-native speakers, slow down, repeat key concepts in different ways and give long pauses. And be careful about the language you use and how you use it – especially when working in a different culture from your own.

Examples

- *The British English expression 'to be perfectly honest' means little other than emphasis that you are expressing a difficult point of view. A German colleague, having translated these words literally, asked: 'Does that mean you usually lie?'*

- *British speakers often favour dramatic understatement (meiosis), saying, for example, 'I'm a bit disappointed' to mean 'I am absolutely furious'. This is hard for a non-native speaker to interpret.*

- *Each language has its own idioms, sometimes based on unfamiliar metaphors. A wide-ranging, non-specific conversation is often described in British English as 'chewing the cud'. How many speakers of business English will know the word 'cud' and that the metaphor alludes to the constant movement of their mouths?*

- *Just because someone says 'yes', it does not mean you have agreement. In some cultures, yes means 'not no' and no may not be socially acceptable. In others, yes may signal weak intent and only corroborating evidence will give you the confidence you need. In some countries, like Japan and the Middle Eastern nations, the word 'no' is rarely used for cultural reasons: in Japan it is seen as rude and discourteous, while in Arab culture, it results in the risk of losing face.*

In complex mixed cultures with people of many backgrounds, it is simplistic and tokenistic for stakeholder managers to match people on the basis of race or some other obvious characteristic. It is most effective to match people based on personality.

chapter 3

More than Just Power: Analysing Your Stakeholders

If you were a pure pragmatist, you would need to engage with stakeholders for one reason: human beings have power over one another and can influence each other's behaviours. In a chapter of the 1959 book *Studies in Social Power*, edited by Dorwin Cartwright, John French and Bertram Raven contributed the first systematic analysis of the ways in which people use power in social situations. Their chapter, 'The Bases of Social Power', created a language for exploring the ways that stakeholders can impose their will on people and events.

At the heart of French and Raven's thinking is the notion that the basis of power lies in the relationship between the person or group that is exerting the power and the person or group over whom they are exerting it. The relationship confers social power, which has multiple sources that they call 'power bases'. In their original work, they identified five of them. Of these five power bases, four clearly refer to power in the sense of an ability to impose your will, so we will start with these.

The first, 'reward power', is the ability to give or withhold a reward that the other person desires and is the direct equivalent of Etzioni's utilitarian power (which we saw in Chapter 1) at the organisational level. Its direct opposite, the ability to impose sanctions, is 'coercive power', which not only matches but also shares a name with Etzioni's organsational equivalent. These two can be seen as the two sides of the same coin.

Coercion is clearly the last resort of a bully and has no place in a modern workplace within an open, democratic society.

Where rewards and punishment are administered fairly, according to a set of agreed rules by someone whose position of authority is widely recognised as deserved, French and Raven describe this as 'legitimate power'. This legitimacy is most often based on hierarchical position, but can also stem from a sense of reciprocal obligation (you did this for me, so I now recognise your right to do that), from equity and fairness (you contributed that, so therefore it is fair that you can ask for this) or from responsibility (calling upon our sense of duty towards a person or group).

The fourth form of social power is 'expert power', which arises from the investment we put in to gain the depth of knowledge and skills that give us the intellectual or technical authority to direct others. Superior knowledge and skills will lead others to defer to our guidance. Later, French and Raven distinguished this from 'information power', which is more about the ability to deploy information effectively, arguing rationally and credibly. With this distinction, however, they started to introduce another element into social power: influence.

I would define 'influence' as the ability to affect other people's attitudes and behaviours. So while the concepts of influence and power are deeply intertwined and are used almost interchangeably by French and Raven, when we set out to analyse stakeholders, we need the subtlety to draw a distinction between the two. As I indicated above, I regard power as the ability to impose your will over people or events.

DEFINITIONS

Power: the ability to impose your will over people or events.

Influence: the ability to affect other people's attitudes and behaviours.

French and Raven's fifth original power base is 'referent power' – the power that stems from the person or group itself (to whom the power refers, hence the name). In an individual, referent power is best understood as personal power that arises from those hard-to-define traits like character, personality, charisma, gravitas and integrity. Your ability to build and maintain relationships and to use those relationships to influence and inspire is your referent power and we can see how information power can flow directly from this. In the group sense, referent power bears a close analogy to Etzioni's normative power in which shared beliefs and values drive compliance.

It is worth noting in passing that other power bases have been identified in the years since French and Raven first coined the term, and two of them will be of particular relevance to us as we analyse our stakeholders: 'connection power', which arises through our ability to harness a network of relationships with other people and groups; and 'resource power', which derives from our privileged access to valuable resources that others want or need, giving us the reward or coercive power to grant access to others or to withhold it.

In understanding power bases, then, we immediately start to understand that there is more to stakeholders than simply power, and this chapter is all about this extra depth. But we will start where all analysis should start by looking at the broad outlines. Before embracing the complex subtleties, let's sort out our stakeholders to gain a simple perspective of who we have and what their characteristics are.

Stakeholder triage

In hospital casualty departments, triage is a prioritisation process of spotting the urgent from among the variety of cases presented. Triage comes from the French word *trier* (to sort).

At the start of our stakeholder analysis, we want to both sort out what we have to understand it better and start the process of prioritisation so that we can focus our energies on what matters most. As with an accident and emergency department, our triage needs to home in on a vital few characteristics that offer the most diagnostic insight.

Different practitioners and their books, articles and practices will emphasise different factors to use in this process. The most common approach is very definitely to focus on 'power' and 'interest': the extent to which stakeholders can impose their will over your project and their level of concern with the project, and therefore their likely incentive to exert their power. We shall return to this particular analysis later on in this chapter, but it is not my preferred starting place.

I recommend an approach that has two principal advantages over the 'standard' approach. First, it recognises the distinction between power and influence, and that both are important. Instead of power, we shall concentrate on 'impact'. This is the ability that a stakeholder has to affect the realities of the world through either power or influence.

Interest tells us something about the level of concern, but nothing about its nature. We will use 'attitude' instead. This is the emotional state that accompanies the interest or level of concern that a stakeholder has. It can range from supportive to opposing and can incorporate a measure of degree. High interest may reflect strong opposition or strong support. With attitude as our second primary characteristic, these are separated, and neutral concern can sit in the middle.

The second advantage of my approach over the standard one is that we shall see that it reveals four immediate strategies for engaging constructively with your stakeholders. Other pairings of factors do not so readily translate into usable approaches.

DEFINITIONS

Impact: the ability to affect the realities of the world through power or influence.

Interest: the level of concern with the project.

Attitude: the emotional state that accompanies the stakeholder's interest or concern.

We perform our stakeholder triage by charting impact against attitude on a simple two-by-two matrix, as illustrated below. Note that, because triage is a first sorting of priorities, we can blithely simplify the world into four boxes, knowing that we will re-introduce all of the complexities later on.

A great way to conduct a robust triage is to gather a small, diverse group of colleagues and work through your stakeholder list, allocating each stakeholder to a position on the chart. A flipchart and sticky notes make a good interactive tool. You can use different-coloured notes for

Low Impact Positive Attitude	High Impact Positive Attitude
Low Impact Negative Attitude	High Impact Negative Attitude

FIGURE 3.1   Stakeholder triage – quadrants

different groups of stakeholders, you can allocate a 'car park' space for the unknowns, and you can put notes on the boundary between supporters and opposers, where the stakeholder is thought to be either neutral or in a 'don't know' state of not having made up their mind. This is an excellent team involvement activity as well as a good way to start your stakeholder analysis.

When the group struggles to place a stakeholder on the chart, this can be due to a number of causes:

- The stakeholder is poorly defined.
- The stakeholder is an inhomogeneous group with different perceptions or powers within it; the best course is to divide this group up – even if it is into artificial 'supporting' and 'opposing' components.
- There is not enough knowledge in the room to assess the stakeholder: they belong in the car park and you will need to prioritise information gathering.
- Some members of the group know something that others don't and your facilitation process needs to allow time for a full discussion of the different points of view.
- The nature of the stakeholder is too complex for a simplistic allocation into one of four boxes and you will need to prioritise a more detailed analysis.

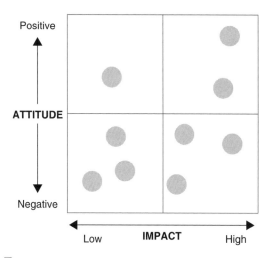

FIGURE 3.2 Stakeholder triage – plotting stakeholders

Whilst the great benefit of a triage process is simplicity, you may choose to move to a next level of sophistication, placing stakeholders at a position in each box that represents the degree of their impact or attitude.

An important tip for anyone conducting this process in a partly public place, or for a public body subject to local freedom of information legislation, is to be cautious with regard to your labelling of the axes. In particular, I would avoid terms like 'supporter' and 'opposer' – and certainly anything less respectful – and would prefer terms that will have less reason to trigger complaint, like 'people and groups that are likely to be supportive' and 'people and groups that are likely to express concerns'. These not only label behaviours rather than positions, but respectfully express them in terms of likelihood rather than certainty.

For some changes and projects, this level of analysis may be sufficient on its own, without the need for further enquiry. You will be able to go straight to planning your engagement campaign from here. Another reason for favouring this approach to triage is that the four boxes give you four simple strategies around which you will be able to build your stakeholder engagement plans.

In Figure 3.3, we see four powerful strategies emerge.

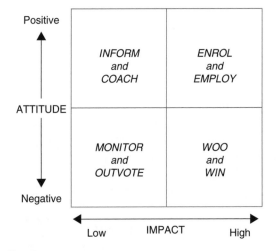

FIGURE 3.3 / **Stakeholder triage**

Woo and win

High-impact stakeholders who oppose what you are doing are likely to be your first priority and your strategy towards them should be clear: you will want to do everything that is lawful and ethical to persuade them of your case. You may not be able to convert them into supporters, but your minimum objective will be to largely neutralise their opposition. These are the stakeholders who can frustrate change or scupper your project.

The reason why this group will be likely to dominate your agenda is the sad nature of human psychology: that we tend to work harder to oppose perceived losses than we do to support gains. We will learn more about this 'loss aversion' in Chapter 6.

Enrol and employ

Those high-impact stakeholders who support what you are doing are valuable assets. This will make them another high priority for you. You need to actively engage their support and use them where you can to help influence the detractors. Their advocacy will be more powerful than your own because of their perceived separation from you and your team.

If they can legitimately be portrayed as objective and disinterested, then their opinions will carry a lot of weight.

Inform and coach

You will also want to use your less impactful supporters to help make your initiative work, but they may need more guidance and coaching as to how they can support you. Give them the information they need and find specific roles where they can help you to be successful, either in influencing other stakeholders or in other ways.

Monitor and outvote

You will feel a strong temptation to ignore those weaker opponents whom you feel can do little to hurt you. They will seem like a low priority at best and a distraction at worst. However, ignoring them would be very dangerous, because you may have misjudged their power or influence, or it may grow while you are not paying attention to them. And, of course, ignoring them would be plainly disrespectful.

Far better would be to keep an eye on them, so that you can re-allocate them and change your strategy if you learn something new: maybe you discover they are friendly with a non-executive director or perhaps you find out that several opposers have linked up and are planning organised action. Now you need to shift them to the bottom-right-hand box and start to pay more attention to them.

Monitor them and invest marginal resources in moving them upwards towards the top-left-hand box. Unlike your high-impact opposers, whom you would meet individually and might respond to with personal letters, you will not have sufficient resources to do this with lower-impact opposers. Instead, you would meet them in larger forums and send them email newsletters rather than personalised messages. If you fail to persuade these stakeholders to support you, this is OK as long as you can outvote them; that is, if their opinions carry too little weight to adversely affect your plans.

The reality of change in complex organisational settings is that there is always the possibility that there will be some losers as a result of the process, no matter how carefully sponsors and promoters have designed the change. If everyone were going to be better off, we'd probably have thought of it and done it a long time ago!

The marginals

There are two forms of marginal stakeholder sitting between opposition and support, which are as follows.

Type 1: floating voters

Floating voters are stakeholders who have not made up their minds. Because they have not decided whether they will support or oppose your initiative, influencing them must be a high priority. Any work you do to engage them will be likely to have a far greater impact than it would for other stakeholders.

Type 2: true neutrals

Some stakeholders are not affected enough by the potential changes – or do not perceive themselves to be – to want to get involved. On the face of it, these will be a low priority to you. But caution is warranted because inappropriate engagement – too little, too much or the wrong approach – may easily alienate them. Persuasion by opposers can also have a profound effect on neutrals. So be sure to give some thought to how you handle neutrals and, at the very least, monitor them.

Analysis framework

Once you have used your triage process to gain an overview of your stakeholders and a simple prioritisation, you may want to enquire more deeply into the nature and characteristics of your stakeholders. The chart on the next page summarises the framework of factors you can bring into your analysis.

It is important to note that you will rarely if ever want to consider more than a handful of these. Select those that are most relevant and that are likely to give you the greatest appreciation of how you can productively engage with your stakeholders to achieve your goals.

D1: Understand the nature of their stake

- Interests
- Needs
- Special needs
- Wants
- Rights
- Ownerships and other control over resources
- Consequences

What is their agenda?

D2: Understand the intensity of their stake

- Attitude
- Impact
- Influence
- Power
- Connection power
- Interest
- Commitment
- Partisanship
- Legitimacy
- Urgency

What is their priority/saliency?

D3: Understand their background and attitudes

- What is their past behaviour?
- Prior experience
- Prior knowledge and information
- Current opinions
- Expectations
- Preferences
- Prejudices
- Motivations
- Values

What do we know about the way they tick?

D4: Additional factors for groups

- Internal dynamics
  - o formal/constitutional
  - o structural/operational
  - o informal/political
- Internal dependencies and connections
- Factions
- Key players and positions
- Demographic make-up
- History and background
- Mission, vision and goals
- Values, culture and style
- Strengths and weaknesses

How does the group work?

Questions to ask that will help with planning

Who...

- ... are they? Where do they fit into their organisation?
- ... are they connected with?

What...

- ... resources do they command?
- ... do we want from them?
- ... information will they want from us?
- ... do they want?

How...

- ... do they like to receive information?
- ... do they like to communicate?

What if...

- What risks do they pose to us?
- What opportunities do they offer us?

How can we maximise the value of engaging with this stakeholder?

FIGURE 3.4 Stakeholder analysis

There are four dimensions to consider about each stakeholder:

D1: The nature of their stake.
D2: The intensity of their stake.
D3: Their background and attitudes.
D4: Additional factors that apply to groups.

D1: The nature of their stake

The fundamental question for each stakeholder is 'what is *their* agenda?'. You and your team will start from your knowledge about the stakeholder, but this is limited by your own biases, preconceptions and prejudices. So who else can you ask? Of course, nothing beats getting real data from the stakeholders themselves, so are you able to include some opinion gathering as an early part of your engagement process?

If you don't have access to your stakeholders, then there is a powerful exercise that can give you and your team astonishing insights. It is called 'Perceptual Positions Analysis'. There are three principal positions from which we perceive our world:

First position   How I see the world; my own perceptions. This is 'my' own subjective experience – in this case, that of the change agent seeking to influence a stakeholder.

Second position   How you see the world; your own perceptions. This is 'your' subjective experience – in this case, that of the stakeholder.

Third position   How 'they' see the world. This is the objective observation of how the stakeholder and the change agent interact.

PERCEPTUAL POSITIONS ANALYSIS

This is easier to facilitate for someone else, but you can do it for yourself. The first thing to do is to set up the room with three of the four sides marked out as: 'me' or 'us'; 'you' or the stakeholder's name on the opposite side; and 'objective observer' on a third wall, at right angles.

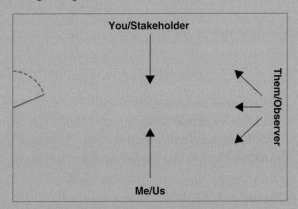

FIGURE 3.5   Perceptual Positions Analysis – set-up

Facilitate the process by asking your collaborator or team to stand on the 'me' or 'us' side of the room, facing the stakeholder side, and say something like the following, pausing after each question to allow people to think through their responses:

> You may want to close your eyes, to help this work really well. You are yourself, standing in your own shoes. Imagine you are facing [your stakeholder] in a typical situation. What do you notice about them? What are their concerns and interests? What do they need from this project? And what do they want from it? What would constitute a big win for them? What attitude do they take with you and what does this indicate?

Give this plenty of time and then ask people to open their eyes, relax and then move to the other side of the room, into the stakeholder space, looking back to where they have just been. Again allowing plenty of time between questions, say something like this:

> You may want to close your eyes again. Now you are [your stakeholder], standing in their shoes. Allow yourself to adjust your posture a little, to feel a little more like them. As [your stakeholder], what are you thinking? What is important to you? How do you feel about [this project]? What outcomes do you need most? What else do you need? What else would you like to have happen as a result? What do you need to avoid? What are you keeping to yourself?

When you have given this plenty of time, ask people to open their eyes, relax and now move to the third side of the room, in the observer space, looking towards the 'me' or 'us' place and the stakeholder place, so that they can observe the interaction. Again allowing plenty of time between questions, say something like this:

> You may want to close your eyes again. Now you are an objective observer, noticing [your stakeholder] and yourself. How are they interacting? What do you notice about [your stakeholder]? What do their concerns appear to be? What is the other person not noticing? What would people around you tell you that they can see? Is there anything [your stakeholder] is not telling the other person?

At the end of this part, tell people to open their eyes and relax, and then make some notes about the insights they have experienced. If you have been working with more than one person, ask them to share their perceptions about your stakeholder and facilitate a discussion. Finally, document what you need to.

The Perceptual Positions Analysis is, of course, a way of tapping into intuitions and knowledge that are held at a subconscious level. Whilst the level of insight can sometimes be startling, you must bear in mind that it can also be wrong. It will be based on your own experiences of the stakeholder, which may be selective and during which the stakeholder may not have shown you all aspects of their agenda. Your experiences and your interpretations of them can introduce bias, so your plans must allow for constant re-evaluation of your analysis against new evidence as it emerges.

Let us consider the different elements that can contribute to a stakeholder's agenda.

Interests

We can define interests as the things that concern a stakeholder, such as financial, political, social, technical, moral and ethical, commercial, regulatory, environmental or security interests. These will be the things upon which stakeholders will base their decisions.

WISE WORDS FROM REAL PRACTITIONERS

Be very open about differences in interests between your stakeholders. What to one stakeholder may be a minor inconvenience may be a catastrophe to another. The same asymmetry is true both of threats and of benefits.

Needs, special needs and wants

Needs and wants are easy to mix up, but the distinction is usually an objective one. This won't matter to the stakeholder who perceives a want as a need. We use the term 'special needs' to refer to those needs that are characteristic of a stakeholder because of who they are rather than what they do or the choices they have made. As an example, a stakeholder who is a salesperson needs information, samples, marketing literature and good communication with logistics and dispatch teams. If they are a wheelchair user, their special needs may include adaptations to their vehicle, modified access to their place of work and increased storage at low levels.

Rights, ownerships and other forms of control over resources

Part of any stakeholder's agenda will be their desire to protect and exert any rights they believe they have. You may want to think about whether you can usefully exploit any responsibilities that accompany these rights. For example, public rights of access over farmland are predicated on responsibilities to enjoy that land without damaging crops, harming livestock or placing yourself or others in danger by tampering with farm equipment. Many rights stem from ownership, which also gives a stakeholder significant control over your options. They may also have control over access to resources, people or information that you need. In this case, you will need to consider how to motivate them to grant you that access.

Consequences

What is the impact of what you are doing on the stakeholder you are considering? The nature and severity of this impact will almost certainly shape their response.

CASE STUDY

A practitioner was preparing a commercial tender for a multi-million pound technology outsourcing contract at an early stage in his career. As project manager, he had such a poor relationship at a senior level that daily, when he met the lead client, he would find himself on the receiving end of shouting and verbal abuse.

The project manager tried to manage the situation by working harder to deliver to the highest possible standards. The result was an exceptional piece of work, but a relationship that never worked well.

In retrospect, the project manager assessed that his failure was to address the client's behaviour and get to the root cause, which was likely to have been a combination of insecurity and mistrust of a younger, less experienced, but talented professional. The project manager missed the opportunity to look for a win-win dialogue where he and his client could look for explicit ways to help one another to succeed.

D2: The intensity of their stake

Attitude and interest

We considered these earlier in the chapter and have defined them already. We also considered why floating voters will give you more bang for your engagement buck. Sitting on a fence is unstable and it is easy to fall one way or the other, so it takes minimal effort to dislodge an undecided stakeholder – for you or for your critics.

Impact, influence and power

We have also already defined impact, influence and power, and have seen how impact is a combination of the other two. We have also talked about the sources of power as arising from one or more power bases. One of these was connection power – sometimes called network power. This allows us to borrow power from the people we are connected to. When we do this with integrity, we ask them for their help. Sometimes, a stakeholder will borrow power without permission (I think that's called stealing) and use someone else's authority in speaking for them. If you detect a stakeholder borrowing authority, it is worth checking whether they have the consent to do so. If you catch them out on this, it will give you some measure of moral power over them, but use this with care: aggrieved and wounded, they may lash out in search of revenge.

Stakeholders with power may try to wield it to sabotage your endeavour, finding fault with what you do, not meeting commitments, withholding information, speaking against you, undermining your authority or trying to compete with you in some way. We will consider how to handle such saboteurs in Chapter 7.

Commitment, partisanship, legitimacy and urgency

Four further things to consider when analysing your stakeholders are the following:

Commitment	The extent to which the stakeholder is committed to their agenda.
Partisanship	The level of impartiality or interest that a stakeholder has.
Legitimacy	How appropriate the stakeholder's involvement is.
Urgency	How urgently you need to respond to the stakeholder.

D3: Their background and attitudes

The more you know about what makes you stakeholder tick, the better you will be able to design your engagement plan to achieve your goals. Some of this will be a matter of record, such as past behaviours, their prior experiences and maybe aspects of their opinions. Other aspects may require judgement on your part, and opinions held by members of your team will differ.

Some people keep their expectations, preferences, values and motivations very much to themselves and any inferences you draw from them will be provisional at best. However, with the highest-priority stakeholders, it may make sense to keep an ongoing confidential record of events and interactions that gives you clues to these subtle personality factors. The most important thing to appreciate is that everyone is different, so think about how you will be able to tailor your communication style to each stakeholder's preferences and personality.

D4: Additional factors that apply to groups

Compared to individuals, stakeholder groups have extra internal dimensions. You need to understand how the group works and therefore how best to engage and influence it. Such factors include the following.

Internal dynamics

How is the group organised and are there any formal structures? If so, how are they constituted and what are the governance procedures that the group must adhere to? Informally, how does the group work at a political level, and what factions and internal groupings are there?

Operational processes

How does the group get things done? Who are the key people and what are the key positions that control decisions and make things happen?

The soft stuff

What are the values, culture and style that exert subtle influences on how the group operates and interacts with other stakeholders? What is the group's history and how does its background influence attitudes and choices? These may be represented in formal statements of mission, vision and strategic goals, but do these mesh with actual behaviours and decisions? And, finally, what is the influence of the demographic make-up of the group? It may be homogeneous or highly diverse. What are the demographic features (such as age, race and gender) that matter in terms of its choices and actions?

Assessment

You may want to assess the group for its strengths and weaknesses, and its likely choices.

Questions

Table 3.1 below also suggests some simple (to ask) questions that will help you to maximise the value of your stakeholder engagement. These will supplement all of the analysis given above and may provide you with further insights.

Table 3.1   Summary of questions to ask about your stakeholders

Who...
• ... are they? Where do they fit in their organisation?
• ... are they connected with?

What...
• ... resources do they command?
• ... do we want from them?
• ... information will they want from us?
• ... do they want?

How...
• ... do they like to receive information?
• ... do they like to communicate?

What if...
• What risks do they pose to us?
• What opportunities do they offer us?

Apex stakeholders

Some of the stakeholder characteristics we looked at above will have a greater influence on the level of priority you assign to a stakeholder. For me, the 'Big Six' stakeholder characteristics are as follows:

1. Interests
2. Needs
3. Attitude
4. Impact
5. Power
6. Influence

One component above all seems to me to dominate and it may seem surprising that it is not power, but influence.

A small number of stakeholders can influence many other stakeholders, yet seem themselves to be very little influenced by other stakeholders around them. They are therefore hard to influence, but can create a lot of leverage if you can do so. They are your 'apex stakeholders'.

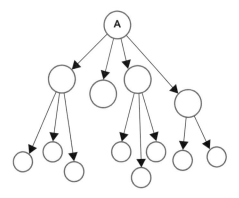

FIGURE 3.6 Apex stakeholders

There will not always be an apex stakeholder, but if there is, you must give them a lot of attention. Indeed, one might define three forms of apex stakeholder:

- *Apex supporters*, who could become powerful allies and advocates.
- *Apex agonists*, who are potentially dangerous enemies.
- *Apex neutrals*, who can be persuaded either way.

Primary stakeholders

'Primary stakeholders' are readily influenced by others (unlike apex stakeholders), but not necessarily by an apex stakeholder; their sources of influence are different. Like apex stakeholders, however, they are good at influencing others and can therefore have a significant impact on perceptions.

Secondary stakeholders

'Secondary stakeholders' are readily influenced by apex and primary stakeholders. They have an important role to play in the project and may have limited influence over others.

Basal stakeholders

Easily influenced with changeable views, 'basal stakeholders' tend to go with the flow of opinion and so are unreliable. They are particularly dangerous if they have a small but vital part to play, such as controlling access to a single important resource.

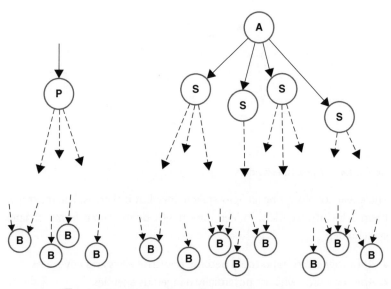

FIGURE 3.7 / Apex, primary, secondary and basal stakeholders

DIFFUSION OF INNOVATION AND THE IMPORTANCE OF OPINION LEADERS

How do new ideas spread? This was a question answered by Dr Everett Rogers in one of the most influential social science books of all time, *The Diffusion of Innovations*. Initially studying how farmers in Iowa adopted new ideas, Rogers examined a wide range of studies about how new ideas and technology diffuse through society, going back to the work of Gabriel Tarde in 1890.

It had long been known that the adoption of ideas follows an 'S Curve', with slow adoption at first, followed by a period of rapid adoption and then a final stage where the remaining people and groups adopt the idea slowly.

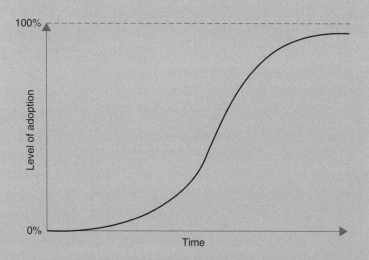

FIGURE 3.8 / **Diffusion of an idea through society**

Rogers identified five stages in the adoption process:

1. Knowledge of the idea, practice or technology that is perceived as new.

2. Persuasion by external sources, through different communication channels.

3. The decision to reject or adopt the idea.

4. Implementation of the new idea or practice (if the decision is to adopt).

5. Confirmation that the adopter will continue to make use of the innovation.

Today, Rogers is most commonly known for his astute coinage of terms for adopters at different stages of the lifecycle of an idea. In particular, his terms have been widely applied to the adoption of technology, and the term 'early adopters' is frequently used in marketing circles.

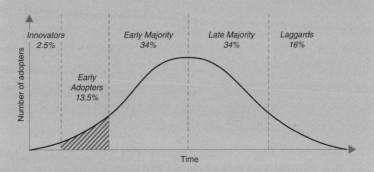

FIGURE 3.9 / **Roger's model of the diffusion of innovations**

The first thing to note is that the very first adopters, the 'innovators', are rarely influential in driving adoption by others. They are often seen as outsiders – in modern technology adoption terms, as 'geeks' – and so have little influence. Innovators do, however, provide a first test of the idea and they can be more tolerant of minor failures, offering you a way to refine and build momentum around an idea.

It is the 'early adopters' who are highly influential. Early adopters are far more socially connected and respected. Unlike innovators, they readily become opinion leaders and may well include your apex stakeholders.

The 'early and late majority' are so called for their impact on adoption rates. By the time that the early majority have adopted an innovation, it has a critical mass of support – 50 per cent of the population. The 'laggards' are the slowest adopters, who may never fully embrace the innovation, but by then, they are at worst a vocal minority of low-influence resisters and at best will display a silent resignation towards the innovation.

An interesting debate amongst historians is the balance of influence over major events between the general currents of history and the impact of key individuals. Rogers' work suggests that, in the context of innovations, whilst opinion leaders can have a big impact on events, change is often well underway by the time they engage with events.

How to handle apex stakeholders

Find your apex stakeholders

People will know who your apex stakeholders are, so ask them... Ask colleagues to make a list of the people who are most influential, most independently minded, most admired and most respected. The names that come up again and again are your apex stakeholders.

Apex stakeholder strategy

Because of their sense of independence, it is not a simple task to influence apex stakeholders; they will not be easily persuaded. You do need to build their trust and tap into their thinking by allowing them to share their ideas and concerns. You must ensure that you make use of their contributions, responding to their ideas and embracing those that have merit.

When an apex stakeholder shows enthusiasm for your initiative, shower them with support and offer resources to help them make your case for you. Keep this appropriate of course – not just for the sake of due propriety, but because you do not want to offend their perception of their independence of mind.

When you are able to influence apex stakeholders, you become the apex stakeholder and can dictate the agenda of many of your stakeholders.

A word of caution

Rogers' early adopters form over 13 per cent of the population: true apex stakeholders will be far fewer. They are therefore not a panacea for communicating a positive message. The large mass of early and late majority and many early adopters must be receptive to the idea, so you will also need to invest your efforts in other ways of engaging them and priming them for your message.

Relationships among stakeholders

The image above of how apex stakeholders influence others gives a linear view of stakeholder relationships that is far from realistic. In reality, the network of stakeholder relationships is far more complex and messy.

All stakeholder engagement is political in the widest sense of the word.

> **DEFINITION**
>
> *Political*: relating to the complex set of relationships among people and groupings within a culture, society or organisation, often involving the exercise of authority or power.

You therefore need to be concerned about the political environment of your programme or change: how do the relationships among stakeholders affect you and what are the patterns of influence that can support or undermine you?

> **WISE WORDS FROM REAL PRACTITIONERS**
>
> *Individual stakeholder reactions are not the whole story: it is also about how they interact. People are not independent of their context, or of one another, and behave differently in groups compared to how they are on a one-to-one basis.*

Stakeholder relationship mapping tools

Relationship mapping tools are designed to help you visualise the connectedness between stakeholders. This will help you to understand who can influence whom to evaluate both threats and opportunities.

Sociograms

The simplest way to map relationships is with a 'sociogram', sometimes called a 'social network diagram'. A simple example from an office move project is illustrated below in Figure 3.10.

In this chart, all of the stakeholders are represented as nodes, with connections between them shown by lines. Stakeholders are clustered in a crude representation of the organisational proximity, but this may not match all of the forms of influence.

We can enhance the amount of information we put into our sociogram by using arrows to depict the direction of influence, so that if A primarily influences B, then the arrow points from A to B. If A and B can equally

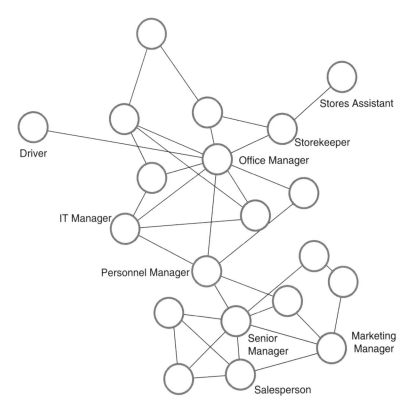

FIGURE 3.10 Basic sociogram

influence one another, then we can use a double arrow. We can also use line thickness to indicate the strength of relationships or level of influence, with a thicker (or double) line indicating a stronger link. Finally, we can also use the symbol for the node to carry more information. For example, a larger symbol can indicate the level of authority or power, you can colour-code the symbol to represent the level of support or opposition for your initiative, and the shape of the symbol could indicate either the attitude as either supportive or antagonistic. These are just examples – choose a representation system that carries the information that is useful to you and avoid the temptation to try to be too clever and include more information than is useful.

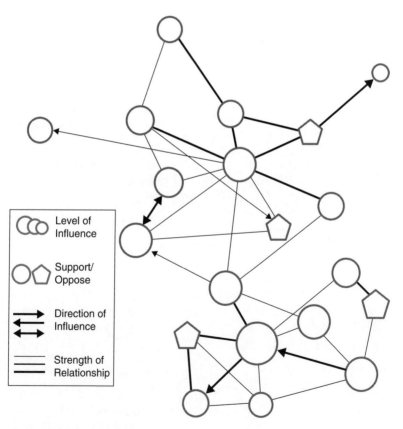

FIGURE 3.11 / Enhanced sociogram

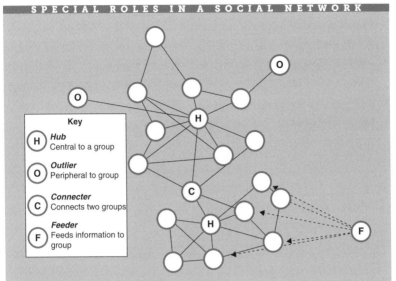

FIGURE 3.12 Typical sociogram structure

In the typical sociogram structure, we can identify some special positions representing roles that some members of the network will often play, labelled H, C, F and O.

Hub (H)

The hub is central to a group and often has substantial influence over them, due to the high degree of social connectedness. Apex stakeholders often show up as a hub.

Connector (C)

Connectors link two or more largely discrete groups on the sociogram. Like hubs, they are well connected, but often have less influence than a hub stakeholder. Their influence comes from their ability to spread ideas or, perhaps more importantly, perceptions about ideas. A connector who links directly to a hub stakeholder can amplify the hub's influence by communicating it to another group.

Feeder (F)

Feeders may be outsiders to a group but have good connections into it. Where a feeder has strong relationships and strong opinions, they can influence a group. Experts are often feeders – they keep to themselves for much of the time, but when they have something important to say, a lot of people listen. Hence, the links in the diagram are shown as one-way.

Outlier (O)

Outliers are also peripheral to a group, but their connections are much weaker. Where you need to influence an outlier, you have to do so directly, and they will be of little help in relaying a message. Many geeks occupy outlier positions, with far less influence than a feeder.

Cassandra

In mythology, Cassandra was a Trojan princess granted the gift of foresight and the curse of never being believed. Cassandras have deep insight, but are rarely listened to and hence often occupy an outlier position in a sociogram. However, many 'false Cassandras' occupy feeder positions. These people are dangerous because their insights are rarely accurate.

Issue inter-relationship map

A variation on a sociogram will allow you to visualise how different stakeholders cluster around the issues within your project. This kind of chart is useful when a project or initiative has a number of issues that are independent of one another, so that a stakeholder may take an interest in some issues, but not others. The chart lets you see which stakeholders follow which issues and also shows you the stakeholders who have a commonality of interests.

To create an 'issue inter-relationship map', start by arranging your issues (labelled 1–4 in Figure 3.13 below) so that related issues are closer to one another than they are to independent issues. Then arrange stakeholders (labelled A–M), showing their interest in various issues as arrows.

Contractual relationships

Large complex projects involving many suppliers, contractors and subcontractors can leave you wondering, day-to-day, who is contracted to whom. I have found it very helpful to draw up a sociogram focused entirely on these contractual relationships – a 'contractogram', if you will.

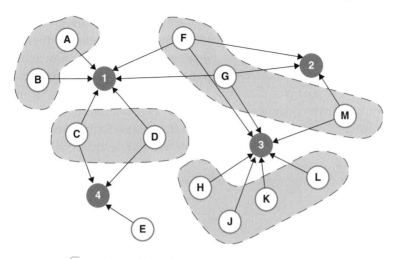

FIGURE 3.13 / Issue inter-relationship map

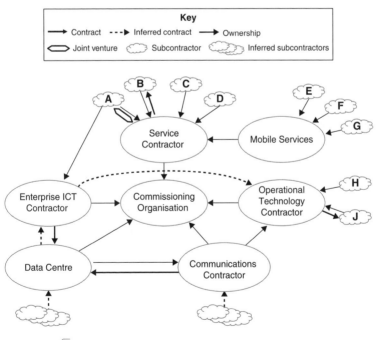

FIGURE 3.14 / Contractogram

Contracts are obviously mutual arrangements, but I use the arrow to indicate the direction of provision of the goods or services that determined the need for the contract, with the balancing payments being implied. Often there are numerous contracts between two parties – and some work in opposite directions, so the figure shows this. I use dotted lines to indicate an inferred contractual relationship, about which I have no formal knowledge, but which I suspect to exist. The strong thick line represents a formal joint venture between two parties and the strong single line represents ownership.

WISE WORDS FROM REAL PRACTITIONERS

Don't map just the individuals, but their key relationships and (formal and informal) group memberships too. Their conversations that they have about you, which you are not part of, are at least as significant as the ones that you can influence at first hand.

Techniques for analysing stakeholders

Perhaps the most obvious approach to analysing your stakeholders is to assign one person to sit at their desk and work through your stakeholder register, assessing each one in turn against a range of factors from the analysis framework. For smaller projects, this is likely to be the project manager or change leader; for larger projects, the project manager or change leader is likely to delegate this to a dedicated stakeholder engagement manager. Whoever does it, they will probably want to start with a triage process to establish priorities and then to work through stakeholders in priority order to create a thorough analysis.

Doing this kind of work alone can be monotonous and lonely, but worst of all, it can lead to a singular perspective that is tainted by one person's perceptions of the world. It is far better for a small group to work together to harness and debate different perceptions. If you want to engage a group of people, why not get them together in an informal workshop setting and go through the process in a structured way?

Stakeholder analysis workshops

A stakeholder analysis workshop is a good way to get a project team working together in the early days of a project or change initiative. It is an event that everybody will be able to participate in, it will make each person feel like a valued part of the team when their opinions are listened to and included, and it will give the whole team a common understanding of a very important facet of your work challenge. In these ways, it is very much like a risk workshop and its structure can, equally, be very similar (see, for example, my book *Risk Happens!*).

If you have a large team, you may want to limit participation in your workshop to make the facilitation process manageable or you may want to consider using a process that splits the large group into smaller units. If you feel that you need to be selective about attendance, prioritise diversity among your selection criteria. The more widely you draw the group, from different disciplines, backgrounds, parts of the organisation or even from different organisations, the broader the range of insights you will have available to work with. Differing opinions may be harder for you, or whoever facilitates, to deal with, but will give a far better result.

Beyond diversity, you are also looking for representation from all parts of the wider team – and maybe from among the various stakeholder groupings. I would also prefer to involve people whom I know to be enthusiastic about the process and the work that will follow it. I will also try to get a balance of analytical, intuitive and emotional thinkers that complements my own style and preferences.

You should also be thinking about the how much time you need to invest in your stakeholder analysis workshop. For a small project, half a day will be plenty. For big organisational changes or contentious community projects, you may need to put aside one or two whole days. If you can undertake a simple triage process, considering the most obvious stakeholders, before planning your workshop, the results will inform you judgement.

Prepare well for your workshop because it is an important event in your programme of work, and how you conduct it can make the difference between a fun, participative and productive event, and a miserable, divisive and disappointing event that is a waste of everybody's time. And, of course, how you run the workshop will frame how people see your management and leadership style, so this is important to you personally. If you are not experienced at facilitating discussions or chairing events like this, you might consider asking someone else to do so, or to help you.

If you have a leadership role, then whether you are leading the workshop or not, take care in terms of how you participate in discussions. It is a well-understood effect that anyone with authority (for example, hierarchical or intellectual) can disproportionately influence the nature of the discussions. This is rarely at a conscious level, but early contributors, especially when they are regarded as highly credible by the group, can often frame the way in which people discuss a topic. A skilled facilitator will be well aware of this and will structure the meeting to mitigate these effects.

Another role for the facilitator is to keep the workshop on track, but to be flexible enough to allow good conversations to continue to a conclusion. They will have ways to deal with conversations that go around in circles or focus in on irrelevant or peripheral issues. A personal favourite of mine for the latter is a simple 'car park' flipchart, where I can write up topics that come up, but which we do not have time to explore at the meeting. This shows the whole group that I have properly understood the issue and have acknowledged its importance. I can then return to our car park at the end of the workshop and decide, with the team, what to do about each item.

The following table gives an indicative agenda that you can adapt to your own needs.

Table 3.2   Indicative agenda for a stakeholder analysis workshop

Opening Session
• Introductions
• Introduce the workshop
• Context and objectives of the change initiative
Stakeholder Identification
Stakeholder Analysis
Stakeholder Engagement Planning
Closing Session
• Next steps review
Follow-up after the workshop

Introductions

Your first priority is to ensure that everybody in the workshop is introduced to one another. Some people favour ice-breaker activities and, if these are well chosen, they can also be a splendid way to get people thinking in the right way – which I would characterise as 'playfully serious and creatively analytical'. For a longer workshop, make the introductions an informal process, maybe over coffee and cake, if you can.

Introduce the workshop

Draw the personal introductions to a clear close and start the business of the meeting by setting out clearly why you have called it, what you want the workshop to achieve, the agenda you propose to follow and what you expect that the participants will get from contributing. If you need to, now is the time to set out any ground rules in terms of how you want people to behave and your expectations of the group.

The context and objectives of the change initiative

Frame the workshop by setting out the context within which the project is operating and the objectives for the changes you will be working together to create. Every participant needs to have a common understanding of your project from the outset and if you have good reference documents, make them available for the team to refer to during the process. I like to put a statement of the goals and objectives up on a wall at this stage so that everyone can easily refer to it.

Stakeholder identification

Use a selection of the techniques covered in Chapter 2 to identify who your stakeholders are. Even if you already have a stakeholder list before the workshop starts, it is well worth repeating the exercise in the workshop. You may get lucky and find some new, possibly important, stakeholders in the process. However, the main reason for doing this is that now the group will feel that the stakeholder list is theirs, and also that, during the identification stage, they will have inevitably started to think about the stakeholders they are identifying. Using the brainwriting technique, you can even run from this agenda item to the next, using the same process.

Stakeholder analysis

Break your stakeholder analysis section into three parts. First get the group to discuss which factors are going to be most useful in analysing stakeholders for your project. In essence, you will be asking them to define 'what makes one stakeholder more important to us than another?' It can be helpful to pick the two most important factors as the basis for a triage.

I would most often use impact and attitude, as described earlier in the chapter.

The second part is to conduct a triage – perhaps using the flipchart and sticky notes approach discussed above. This will give everyone a chance to discuss and debate, and is typically where the workshop gains energy. The two most valuable things you will get from this step are a sense of priorities among your stakeholders and a feel for which ones will require more careful consideration to really understand them.

The third part is to analyse stakeholders in depth. Here you will consider additional factors that provide useful insights into your stakeholders and distinctions between them. This part may need to have time limits imposed on it and may be more productive if the larger group can be split up in some way. But here is where the hard work will be done, thinking through what the team knows and believes about each stakeholder, and how to distinguish between knowledge and supposition. In the next main section of this chapter, 'Stakeholder analysis tools' on page 76, there are a number of different tools that you can use in this section of the workshop, such as force-field analysis, or different forms of stakeholder mapping. You may also want to create maps of stakeholder relationships, such as a sociogram (page 63) or an issue inter-relationship map (page 66).

Be clear in your explanation as to what you want and how you want the group to proceed, and ensure that you have an adequate mechanism to capture the consensus of the group and any outlier opinions. It is equally important – particularly if you are subject to any freedom of information regulations – that the way discussions are documented is appropriate and respectful.

Stakeholder engagement planning

You may have scheduled time to start planning strategies and responses to stakeholders in your workshop, and now is the time to do so. Realistically, this may be too much for one session, so the alternative is to allocate stakeholder owners, particularly to those stakeholders assessed as being highest priority. These people will be tasked with coming up with first draft plans that can be collated and reviewed. If you do this, ask them for a commitment to specific actions or progress by a specific deadline. On the other hand, you may want to take the results of your analysis back to the office and task a single person or a small group with building a strategy around it.

Next steps review

End your workshop with a summary of what the team has agreed, what actions each person has committed to, and the next steps for you and for the team. The final thing you should do in the workshop is thank your colleagues for their contributions.

Follow-up

Follow up your workshop within 24 hours with a written note, repeating your thanks, re-stating the commitments that each person made, and laying out the next steps.

Stakeholder role play

Near the start of this chapter (page 50), I offered a powerful tool for gaining insight into the nature of a stakeholder's stake: the Perceptual Positions Analysis. You can adapt this for a wider analysis of important stakeholders and it can fit well into a stakeholder analysis workshop.

A more informal approach is to ask members of your workshop group to each play the role of one stakeholder or stakeholder group. They should review whatever analysis is already available from earlier group work and should then think of themselves as that stakeholder or a representative of the group. Put questions or scenarios to your 'virtual stakeholder group' and get their responses. You might suggest a scenario for how changes or disruptions can be managed and ask what impact this would have on them and how they feel about them. You might ask them what solutions would work best for them or what they want to achieve. Encourage the virtual stakeholders to debate amongst themselves to look for solutions that balance their interests. Ensure that you have some impartial observers who can capture what arises and feed prompts and provocations back into the group. Once you have set up this sort of exercise well, it can take on a life of its own and go in many different directions.

Stakeholder meetings and interviews

If in doubt, ask your stakeholders for their opinions. Sometimes this will be inappropriate, but often it is a powerful way to get them fully engaged in the process. You can do this in individual interviews, in small focus groups or in larger stakeholder group meetings.

One practitioner particularly favours 'stakeholder forums' – regular (fortnightly) early-morning meetings with a diverse cross-section of the organisation. The group is skewed towards outsiders, mavericks, sceptics and objectors. Over coffee and muffins, the engagement manager holds town hall conversations that get information out to the stakeholders, gather genuine feedback and concerns, and act as an early warning system. The process also places any perceived troublemakers 'inside the tent'.

Before you meet your stakeholders, you must prepare well, knowing what you need to achieve and doing your homework to know as much as is publicly available about that stakeholder. Avoid asking questions to which their reply would be 'you should know that'. At the start of my career as a consultant, I made exactly this mistake. Interviewing a senior stakeholder, I asked too many questions to which he felt I should have already known the answer. He terminated the interview before I could learn anything useful.

I have since found that a structured interview with pre-prepared questions helps to ensure that I get the answers I need, and the discipline of writing notes as I go ensures that I can recall it. If you need to, simply say: 'That is an important point, thank you. Would you mind if I just write some notes before I ask my next question?' I also like to think about where to hold an interview. Going to your stakeholder's desk or workstation, or letting them choose the location tends to put them most at ease and is more respectful. If you summon them to your desk, it asserts a power that you may have, but think carefully before deploying it.

Remember that an interview is a social thing, so start with introductions and a little rapport building rather than diving straight in. Set out why you wanted to meet and what you want to achieve. Ask your stakeholder what they want to get out of the interview. At the end, I always ask my 'final question', which will be something like 'is there anything else I should have asked you?' or maybe 'is there anything else you would like me to make a note of?'. These questions ensure that your stakeholder gets the last word and also places the responsibility onto them for any essential information that you did not know to ask about.

I typically follow up an interview by typing up my notes and sending them for comment and amendment to the interviewee. I want them to know that I value accuracy and that I recognise that my notes are, at best, my understanding of what they tried to convey. And, of course, I want to get it right and be transparent about what I have recorded. I will always thank my stakeholder for their time at the end of the interview and again in writing afterwards, and if I have made any promises, I am scrupulous in following these up.

In focus groups or larger stakeholder meetings, apply the same principles, but spend even less time talking and more time listening to the banter among your stakeholders.

Questionnaires

Another way of getting information from stakeholders is a questionnaire. This is appropriate when you have large numbers, can characterise the questions clearly, and the stakeholders you want to survey are towards the lower end of the range of importance to you. The large numbers are necessary because compliance rates are often low and some deliberately disruptive answers can skew statistics badly in a small survey sample. The lack of subtlety and follow-up means that your questions have to be precise and the range of answers that you allow for must be completely exhaustive, so test the survey on a sample of stakeholders to ensure that it works. The big problem is that a questionnaire is a shortcut, so only use it where stakeholders cannot reasonably take offence at this approach or, if they do, you will not mind too much.

The Internet offers a wide range of low-cost and free tools to support you in this. But don't be a cheapskate: if you are spending $20 million on a corporate change programme, picking a visually poor survey tool that does not allow the answer types you need just because it is free and so you don't need to get approval for the contract is a false economy.

LABELLING STAKEHOLDERS

In analysing stakeholders, it is tempting to put neat labels on certain groupings. Many authors and consultants have, indeed, come up with compelling terminology that can be a lot of fun for the team on the inside, but that can also be alienating to others – and even disrespectful. So adopt labels with great caution.

Labels fall into two classes: literal and metaphorical. Largely, it is the metaphorical labels that cause a smile. Let's look at some examples for the fun of it, then agree to keep them out of serious projects, just as doctors would no longer (I hope) use the colourful slang that medical students once learned, like FLK (Funny Looking Kid) or UBI (Unexplained Beer Injury).

Literal labels

Positive: Advocates, Supporters, Adopters, Helpers

Neutral: Opinion formers, Decision-makers, Neutrals, Undecideds, Sceptics

Negative: Opposers, Blockers, Saboteurs, Critics

Metaphorical labels

Positive: Drivers, Fans, Angels, Back-benchers, Friends, Saviours

Neutral: Gate-keepers, Floating voters, Sleeping giants, Fence-sitters

Negative: Stick-in-the-muds, Shadow cabinet, Enemies, Irritants, Oiks

Stakeholder analysis tools

There is a near-infinite variety of tools available, so this section has to be selective. Luckily, the conventions of modern books allow us to be a little more comprehensive without overburdening a chapter with too many alternatives, so you will find a register of eight more tools that I have found helpful over the years in Appendix 3. Here I will focus on those I have found to be the most important. But the selection is personal, so evaluate what you need and choose the best tool for the job.

Adding to your stakeholder register

We discussed your stakeholder register in Chapter 2. At that stage, you would doubtless have done little more than start it off with the names and key characteristics of your stakeholders. Having performed your analysis, you will want to record all of this on your register.

Stakeholder persona cards

The marketing profession offers us an alternative to the stakeholder register. When preparing a large marketing campaign afresh, marketers will identify 'typical' representatives of different parts of their target market so that they can craft well-focused messages for each grouping. This should sound pretty familiar!

What they will often do is create a 'persona' for each ideal customer. This is a realistic representation of a fictional character who is typical of the group, often based on real data from demographic and survey information, coupled with knowledge from focus groups, online behaviours, interviews and sometimes informed speculation.

The personas capture all the relevant information about behaviours, habits, motivations and preferences. Often the team will then give each persona their own profile recorded on an index card.

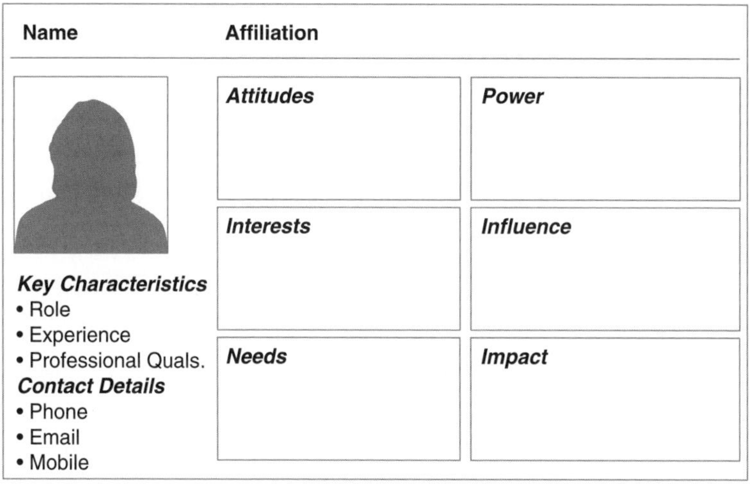

Name	Affiliation	
	Attitudes	**Power**
	Interests	**Influence**
Key Characteristics • Role • Experience • Professional Quals. **Contact Details** • Phone • Email • Mobile	**Needs**	**Impact**

FIGURE 3.15   Persona card

The persona card will record all of the information that the team needs, often with a caricature of the typical person. For yours, you might have a real photo of the stakeholder or a logo for a stakeholder group, but the principle works well.

Some examples of information you may want to record on your persona cards are as follows:

- Persona name and affiliation.
- Key characteristics, such as role, seniority, experience, gender and professional background (note: be careful about recording items such as age, gender or ethnic background that could be used for unethical or illegal discrimination. Always be sure that what you record is pertinent to legitimate choices or real understanding).
- 'Big six analysis' of power, impact, influence, attitudes, needs and interests.
- 'Community of interests': how you can help each other to create a win-win situation.
- Essential messages you need to deliver.
- The stakeholder's preferred communication channels and methods.
- The stakeholder's personality and the way they think – for example, do they take a practical or theoretical approach to problems, are they risk averse or a risk taker, do they like to share opinions or to research independently and do they prefer anecdotal or hard evidence?
- Things they might say: typical quotes or buzzwords.
- Reasons they may support or oppose you.
- 'Influence map': who can influence this persona and who they can influence.
- An assessment of your goals and challenges with respect to the persona.

Stakeholder mapping

Stakeholder mapping describes a whole number of tools that represent your stakeholders as occupying a position on one or more continua, such as power, attitude, influence or commitment. Typically a stakeholder map can represent two or even more of these dimensions.

We map stakeholders to communicate a lot of information in one simple image and, done well, the maps can be engrossing, drawing people in to consider what they mean. This can create a shared understanding and can sometimes generate new insights through spotting patterns. They also invite criticism and challenges, which can further enhance our understanding. Some maps – like the one we used for the triage section (page 46) – also suggest broad strategies or prioritisation of our stakeholders. Let's consider some more.

The 'standard' stakeholder map

Perhaps the form of stakeholder map that you will see most often maps stakeholder power against their interest in what you are doing. You will find this in many places with slight variations.

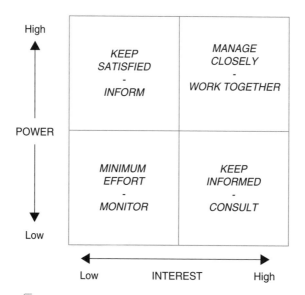

FIGURE 3.16 The 'standard' stakeholder map

This is so ubiquitous that it is often referred to as if it is *the* stakeholder map, but it is one of many approaches. There are other examples in Appendix 3, but here I want to focus on an alternative, which I have developed from the simple triage approach at the start of this chapter.

The Influence Agenda stakeholder map

The Influence Agenda stakeholder map starts, like many others, with four quadrants that indicate either support or opposition and either high or low levels of impact. It introduces a third dimension by dividing each quadrant into an inner and outer zone representing low and high levels of interest in the change in the inner and outer zones respectively. There is also a 'neutral zone' for stakeholders of high or low impact and high or low interest, who are neutral either because they do not have a strong opinion either way (the neutrals) or because they have yet to make up their minds (floating voters) (see page 48).

Each stakeholder can therefore be mapped into one of 12 zones. The figure also shows the overall strategies as arrows, with all but one as positive strategies in the sense that they have integrity. It is worth noting that the additional strategy is negative in the sense that it would demonstrate low integrity in undermining the influence of a stakeholder. It is high risk, but worth mentioning, not because I advocate it – I absolutely do not – but because it is common, particularly among politicians. The broad approaches that these strategies represent for each of the four quadrants are labelled as follows.

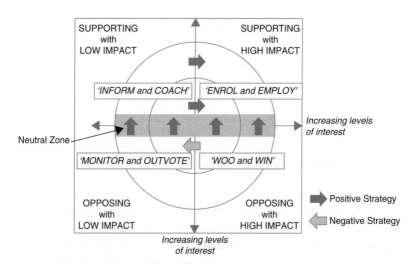

FIGURE 3.17   The Influence Agenda stakeholder map

Woo and win

At lower levels of interest, the strategy is to woo the stakeholders, to understand their issues and use subtler forms of persuasion to reduce the risk that they become more actively engaged in opposing you. At higher levels of interest, you need to actively win over stakeholders and be prepared to use extensive efforts to persuade – anything that is ethical and lawful! Also be prepared to isolate these stakeholders to prevent the contamination of neutrals and be ready to engage with active opposition constructively.

Enrol and employ

You need to increase the level of interest of your high-profile supporters by enrolling them to your cause so that you can harness the support and influence they possess. When they are engaged, find ways to use these motivated and influential supporters.

Inform and coach

Keep these supporters informed, and thus able to help you, and build their enthusiasm. Find ways that they can help you and coach them in how to be useful, whilst also taking advantage of their insights and counsel.

Monitor and outvote

Keep an eye on your low-impact opponents in case they become more engaged or more influential and, if they do, be prepared to shift your strategy accordingly. Keep working to persuade them, but limit your commitment in accordance with their lower impact and therefore priority. However, essentially your strategy must be pragmatic: you may not be able to persuade them easily and your resources will be limited. If they genuinely have low impact, you must be prepared to outvote them using the support that you have, knowing that their voices will carry little weight.

Adding more dimensions to your stakeholder map

The Influence Agenda stakeholder map already has three dimensions: impact, attitude and interest. You could add up to three more dimensions, although I would counsel against it. But if you do want to add any extra information to your stakeholder map, here are three more variables to apply to the symbol you use for your stakeholder:

Shape   For example: triangles, squares or circles; smiley, neutral and sad faces.

Size   For example: small, medium and large.

Colour For example: red, green or blue; blank, shaded or filled.

I do not recommend literal colours alone, as two per cent of the male population is red-green colour blind, as are all black-and-white printers and photocopiers.

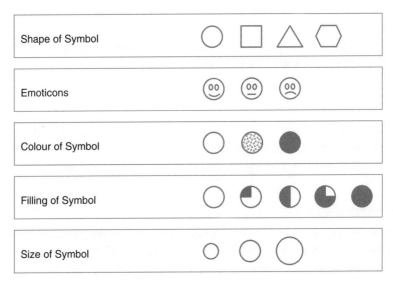

Shape of Symbol	○ □ △ ⬡
Emoticons	😊 😐 🙁
Colour of Symbol	○ ◍ ●
Filling of Symbol	○ ◔ ◑ ◕ ●
Size of Symbol	○ ○ ○

FIGURE 3.18 **Examples of symbols for use in stakeholder maps**

Stakeholder force-field analysis

Stakeholder force-field analysis provides a very simple way to visualise the stakeholder forces on your project. In Figure 3.19 below, you can see that the project is named in the centre, and the supporters and opposers are shown as forces of different strength, pulling in opposite directions. In the figure, I have added neutral and undecided stakeholders too. Counting the bars on the arrows on each side will give you a crude measure of the net support for or opposition to your project.

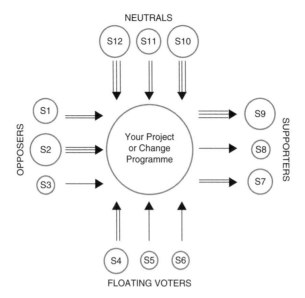

FIGURE 3.19 Stakeholder force-field analysis

Stakeholder engagement strategy planner

Even at the analysis stage, you will want to start thinking about your engagement strategy. For this I recommend a simple planning tool in the form of a table, as given in Template 3.1 below.

Template 3.1   Stakeholder engagement strategy planner

Stakeholder	
What we need or want from them	
What they need or want from us	
Attitude, impact, influence and power	
Background and attitudes	
Strategy to adopt	

You can download a stakeholder engagement strategy planner template from www.theinfluenceagenda.co.uk.

At the centre ...

... is you and your team. It is easy to overlook yourselves in your stakeholder analysis, but there are two reasons why you should not do so:

1. You each have your own attitudes to the changes and your own influence on them. These need to be addressed as part of the stakeholder engagement process. You may be a very particular set of stakeholders, but you are stakeholders nonetheless.
2. You and your team will be managing the stakeholder engagement process and the skills, experience and attitudes you bring will be instrumental. When it comes to planning your action, these will be valuable inputs into your plan and so need to be examined.

So make time to analyse the resources, skills and experience you can bring to bear when you engage with your stakeholders. And also look at the intangible factors that can make a real difference: attitudes, motivation, confidence and commitment.

WISE WORDS FROM REAL PRACTITIONERS

Embrace asymmetry. If everyone genuinely wants the programme to succeed, then it is important to understand the things that might drive behaviour in one party but which another might see as obstructive or counterproductive. With very few exceptions, you will find that people are neither lazy nor malicious – they come to work to do a good job. So if they are doing something unhelpful, it is probably for a good reason. By understanding and actively embracing differences of emphasis, it is possible to chart a better-optimised course through the needs of different stakeholders and to avoid the misery of misunderstandings and disagreements.

4

chapter

What are You Doing?
Crafting Your Message

If your organisation does not tell people as much as they want to know and if it fails to keep communication ahead of events, then in the absence of real information, people will fill the vacuum with rumour. When we find out what is going on through rumour and gossip, we start to lose confidence – we feel as if nobody is in control. Because rumour loves exaggeration and gossip loves alarm, the information we obtain from uninformed sources is always more scary than reality.

In our minds, change plus uncertainty equals conspiracy. Ironically, because of the many theories surrounding his death, this is what US President John F. Kennedy meant when he said: 'The great enemy of the truth is very often not the lie – deliberate, contrived and dishonest, but the myth – persistent, persuasive and unrealistic.'

This leads me to Stakeholder Rule Number 3: *honesty is not the best policy … it is the only policy.*

Remember that, in times of organisational change, a lie is not always a deliberate untruth; it is more often a promise that you do not know, at the time you make it, whether you can keep: 'Everybody will be consulted', 'This will transform our fortunes', 'There will be no redundancies', etc.

Half-truths and spin seem to be a staple for the political classes, but they seem to me to be not just bad practice, but amateurish. Treat people with respect – as you would wish to be treated – and your communication campaign will be far more effective. As in the world of politics, secrets will out. So, to minimise your stress levels and to maximise your credibility, be as open with people as you legally can be.

Uncertainty is often the reason why we hold information back: we don't want to give a partial message only to have to change it later. Again, you can share the whole truth by telling people about the uncertainty because we intuitively grasp the truth of Socrates' assertion that wisdom lies in knowing the limitations of your own knowledge. Being honest and saying 'I don't know' will earn respect.

Respect also requires integrity: a complete consistency between what you say and what you do. People interpret actions as the measure of truth and where these do not match the message of your words, they will not believe you. Your actions are messages, so keep all of your messages consistent.

The basics of communication

Communication often goes wrong. This is not because we intend it to or because we aim to lie, but because it relies largely upon how one person interprets the message of another. Let's break this down into steps.

Communication starts with an idea of my intended message and the outcome I hope to achieve in communicating it. I then communicate, maybe in speech or in another of the hundreds of ways available to me. The person I am addressing will hear or receive my message and will filter it through

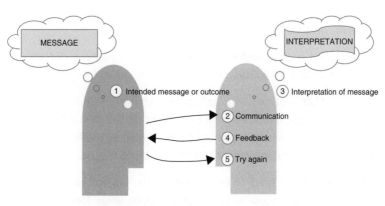

FIGURE 4.1 / **How communication works**

their experiences, their own language patterns and their ways of thinking to create an interpretation of what I said. Usually this interpretation is pretty much what I intended, but sometimes it is not: I have had to put my idea into words, which subtly change it, and my partner's filters have further selected from those words and re-interpreted their meanings to create something new.

Now they respond, and that is the feedback I need to assess the level of correspondence between my intent and their understanding. Finally, if I need to, I can try again. If I want to be sure that someone understands me, I must take responsibility, not just for what I say but also for evaluating their response and changing how I make my point, if I need to.

Successful communication

Taking responsibility for your communication leads to four things you must try to achieve:

1. Craft a message that is clear, consistent and aimed at the right audience. Be aware of the language skills you audience has, and if you are not communicating in their first language, simplify the way you deliver it.
2. Choose a delivery mechanism that meets the needs of your audience. This gives us Stakeholder Rule Number 4: *communicate with people in the way that they like to communicate.*
3. Create a way to test how your audience received your message so that you can assess how well you have communicated.
4. Be prepared to revise your approach accordingly. It is no good blaming me if I don't understand you; if you want me to understand, find a different way of saying it.

WISE WORDS FROM REAL PRACTITIONERS

People are wired differently. Your task is to try to figure out what sort of person they are and what kinds of message will resonate with them so that you can connect with them on their own wavelength. This also allows you to be more targeted and specific in what you communicate.

Getting your message across with impact

Some people will interpret my message about honesty as a need to focus on the facts and nothing but the facts. This is not what I want to convey.

If you want your message to be powerful, the facts are seldom enough. Have you ever tried to persuade someone with facts and you knew you were right, yet they would not be persuaded? As far back as the fourth century BCE, Aristotle codified the three things you need to create a persuasive argument, and hard logic was just one of these.

In communicating well, you need to demonstrate 'ethos', 'logos' and 'pathos': the three musketeers of persuasive communication. Ethos is your character – the reason why I should believe you. We demonstrate this by showing an appreciation of the needs of the stakeholders we are dealing with and by acting with courtesy, confidence and integrity. Logos is your logic and reason – a good argument supported by reliable evidence. Pathos is emotion. We often denigrate the role of emotion in organisational life, yet organisations are made up of people, whose reactions and decisions are largely driven by the way they feel about events. Aristotle knew that to convince stakeholders of an argument, you will need to present them with compelling emotional reasons.

The great Roman lawyer Cicero was well aware of the need to use emotion to move an audience before you can move their minds or their feet. So too are modern advertising professionals, whose first goal is to capture attention and then to stimulate interest. They most often do this by appealing to our emotions so that they can get us into a receptive mood. They then set out their case, hoping to sway our opinion and finally they want us to take action, so they will provide a clear message about how to buy their product. They use the acronym *AIDA*:

Attention   Take control of your stakeholder's attention.
Interest   Use mood and emotions to stimulate interest in your message.
Desire   Deploy an argument, tell a story or show images that will persuade – often with visceral emotions – your stakeholders to want what you are promoting.
Action   Show your stakeholder what to do next to harness their desire.

Questions to ask

Planning your message is essential and to do so, you need to call upon the understanding you gained at the analysis stage. Some of the most valuable questions were listed in Chapter 3 (page 56), which we can recall here:

Who...
- ... are they? Where do they fit in their organisation?
- ... are they connected with?

What...
- ... resources do they command?
- ... do we want from them?
- ... information will they want from us?
- ... do they want?

How...
- ... do they like to receive information?
- ... do they like to communicate?

What if...
- What risks do they pose to us?
- What opportunities do they offer us?

One question will dominate: 'what do they want?' or, to put it another way, 'what's in it for them?'. This leads to one of the most valuable tools for stakeholder engagement: the 'benefits register'.

The benefits register

The benefits register is a tool developed within the programme and change management disciplines. It provides a detailed schedule of the positive outcomes the programme is designed to achieve and is used initially as an important component of your 'business case' and then as a starting point for creating a 'benefits realisation plan'. For stakeholder management, there are two further compelling reasons to develop a comprehensive register of planned benefits:

1. To understand the 'what's in it for me?' factor for each stakeholder.
2. During the delivery of your programme, to plan good news campaigns that will motivate supporters and gainsay the doom-mongers and sceptics.

The tool you can create from the programme's benefits register is a 'stakeholder benefits matrix', as illustrated below.

Template 4.1   Stakeholder benefits matrix

	Stakeholders				
	No. 1	No. 2	No. 3	No. 4	No. 5
Programme benefits					
Benefit 1	wholly	partially		wholly	
Benefit 2	partially		wholly		
Benefit 3		wholly	wholly		
Adverse impacts					
Impact 1					partially
Impact 2		wholly			
Impact 3		wholly			

TOUGH NUTS

Some stakeholders will benefit little from a change – and may even be adversely impacted by it. This would be fine if they had little power or influence, but what if they do have power and know how to use it? For these tough nuts, you need a plan. But what will influence them?

The basic process is to apply the role-play process we saw on page 73, but ask several colleagues, who all know this stakeholder in different contexts, to put themselves in the stakeholder's shoes. Get them to imagine that they are the stakeholder or a member of the group and ask them questions that could reveal a point of influence, such as the following:

- What do you want?
- What is driving your opposition to this project?
- How could you get something valuable from this project?
- What really motivates you?
- What is it you really fear from this change?
- What would make you change your mind about this project?
- Aside from this change, what gives you sleepless nights?
- Who do you trust and listen to?
- What do you know that we don't?
- What do you know that you don't want anyone else to know?

The basis of this exercise is that a lot of our thoughts and fears do leak out and other people can become aware of them – but often at a subconscious level. By relaxing people, taking your time and asking open questions, you can encourage these little snippets of knowledge to cohere into valuable insights.

Strategic intent

Start planning your communication by thinking about the outcome you want and the tone you need to set to achieve it. Will you request or require, inquire or insist, consult or command?

Alternative stakeholder engagement strategies

Many of the strategies you could adopt can be charted onto a two-dimensional grid, with axes that represent the following:

1. A spectrum from withdrawing from your stakeholders to actively seeking to get involved with them.
2. A spectrum from working against stakeholders who oppose you to working with them to achieve your goals.

Figure 4.2 below illustrates this grid and where some of the strategies fall on it.

It is often said that the more you collaborate, the more commitment and 'buy in' you will get. In fact, there are other reasons for collaboration. More involvement from different people can give you more solutions, more robust decision-making and greater scrutiny of ideas. People are also more likely to accept an adverse decision if they believe that it was arrived at through a fair process. So how do you decide what level of engagement, from direction to collaboration, is right for any given stakeholder? The simple questionnaire given in Table 4.1 below will help. This tool will not tell you what strategy to apply, but it will help you to evaluate where on the spectrum you should be considering pitching your approach. You may often choose a combination of these strategies, applying different approaches to different stakeholders.

	Concede	Accommodate	Assist	Coach	Empower	Collaborate
	Appease	Placate	Support	Consult	Involve	Build Coalitions
	Notice Opportunities	Take Opportunities	Look for Opportunities	Engage	Compromise	Negotiate
Avoid	Monitor	Respond	Inform	Accept Feedback	Compromise	Solicit Feedback
	Identify Risks	Guide	Scan for Problems	Marketing	Influence	Negotiate
	Outvote	Counter	Defend	Inducements	Divide & Rule	Persuade
	Over-rule	Manipulate	Dominate	Suppress	Coerce	Attack

COLLABORATE — Working with Stakeholders

ENGAGE — Getting involved with Stakeholders

COMPETE — Working against Stakeholders

AVOID — Withdrawing from Stakeholders

FIGURE 4.2 Range of stakeholder engagement strategies

Table 4.1   Stakeholder engagement strategy questionnaire

Collaboration	Consultation	Direction
❑ How people perceive the process is paramount.	❑ How people perceive the process is important.	❑ How people perceive the process is subordinate to the outcome.
❑ We have done very little thinking and testing of our ideas.	❑ We have thought through and tested our ideas, but need to refine details and create a final level of confidence.	❑ We believe our ideas are thoroughly thought-out and tested.
❑ Commitment from everybody is essential/ highly desirable.	❑ Commitment from everybody is desirable.	❑ Commitment from everybody is not necessary.
❑ Timescales are relaxed, with plenty of time available.	❑ There is a fixed timescale, with a reasonable amount of time available.	❑ We are under tight time pressures.
❑ Our objectives and outcomes are highly flexible.	❑ There is some room for manoeuvre around the detail of our objectives and outcomes.	❑ Our objectives and outcomes are fixed.
❑ Responsibility for success or failure needs to be spread widely.	❑ We need to share some responsibility for success, or failure needs to be spread widely.	❑ We are prepared to take full responsibility for success or failure.
❑ Stakeholders are largely individuals and small groupings.	❑ Stakeholders include mid-sized groups.	❑ Stakeholders include a number of large groupings.
❑ Stakeholders have high levels of interest and are highly motivated to get involved.	❑ Stakeholders have an interest and want to be involved.	❑ Stakeholders have little interest and low motivation to become involved.
❑ We are expecting substantial resistance to our plans.	❑ We anticipate some resistance to our plans.	❑ We anticipate little or no resistance to our plans.
❑ Mature, experienced, expert stakeholders.	❑ Experienced stakeholders with relevant perspectives.	❑ Inexperienced stakeholders.
Total number of ticks:	Total number of ticks:	Total number of ticks:

Choosing your frame

Another way to think about your strategy is to consider how you will frame your relationship with each stakeholder. Frames dictate your agenda, constrain thinking and set the ground for any debate. For example, the 'blame frame' establishes a dialogue about fault. It is rooted in the past and can serve little purpose in either making progress or strengthening the relationship. Your frame will guide both parties towards a common interpretation of what the issue is about. Your stakeholder may not accept the frame, but we know from psychology that when one person starts a dialogue confidently asserting one piece of information or one interpretation, this can create an

Table 4.2   A choice of frames

Frame	Description
Action frame	Focuses on progress and results and concentrates discussion on methods, deadlines and responsibilities.
As-if frame	Assumes that a hypothetical or future situation is real and focuses discussion on the consequences.
Aversion frame	Focuses on avoidance of loss, which is a powerful motivator. Used to show how an option or scenario mitigates losses.
Choices frame	Focuses discussion on the options and on making decisions. Very much future-oriented, creating a sense of control.
Constructive frame	Like the action frame, highly practical, focusing on finding ways to make something work rather than on why it cannot.
Contrast frame	Contrast this with that – focuses on the comparison with alternatives.
Creative frame	Like the constructive frame, focuses on innovation and working to solve a problem with new thinking.
Critical frame	Looks for risks and points of failure to give a feeling that concerns are being respected and incorporated into the process.
Emotive frame	Appeals to emotion and loyalty and allows parties to share their feelings about a situation.
Evaluation frame	Examines data and evidence and then applies rigour and logic. Moves focus away from emotion onto facts.
Evidence frame	Focuses on a search for evidence from all sources and suggests that a final decision has not been made.
Intuitive frame	Open to instincts and feelings to tap into deep experience. This frame is dangerous where participants have low levels of expertise or experience, rendering their intuition faulty.
Outcome frame	Focuses on what the parties want at the very end of a process – the end rather than the means. Use this frame if the process is uncomfortable but the result will yield significant benefits.
Purpose frame	Focuses on the reasons why and counters concerns about the meaning of events. Without an answer to the question 'why', people will resist a change.
Values frame	Sets the discussion to be about what is important or even 'right'.
Vision frame	Establishes the discussion as being about a clearly defined future.

anchor that draws the other person's perspective in that direction. Table 4.2 sets out some positive frames that you could set.

Branding

Many corporate projects, programmes and change initiatives are given a name and sometimes even a logo. Sometimes, for the biggest and most important programmes, organisations even employ marketing or branding professionals to develop these. They give the initiative a personality and, in many ways, set the frame for it. Branding is frame-setting and it communicates a sense of what the project is about and can emphasise one or two high-level features like priorities, values or cultural style. A good logo can communicate valuable information through shape, style and colour.

Of course, this will always be far harder in multinational projects, where colours, images and words do not carry the same connotations in different cultures. The level of investment will therefore need to be greater and you would be wise to test ideas with sample groups before making it public. There is a long and abominable history of projects being given names that later emerged as having unfortunate connotations, like the Campus Real-time Analysis Project (with its problematic acronym), Project Concorde (which was named after the aircraft and was half-completed when the Air France Concorde crashed) and the Babel project (a translation project whose namers forgot that the mythical Tower of Babel was never finished).

Compelling, persuasive and powerful messages

When you come to drafting your message, designing your materials or preparing what you want to say, your aim must be to make it compelling, persuasive and powerful. We will consider each of these in turn: what they mean and how to achieve them.

Compelling

A compelling message is one that first draws stakeholders in and makes them want to read, view or listen further. Second, it must be easy to understand, giving your stakeholders a clear sense that they can grasp the meaning and know what is expected of them. We create a compelling message by giving our communication a good structure, so let's examine three techniques for doing this.

Flow and sequence

Structure how you communicate your message into a simple sequence that your stakeholders can follow easily; for example, step by step, chronological or region by region. Early on, tell readers, viewers or listeners what to expect and, if the message is long, periodically signpost where you are in the sequence. Make sure that there is a logical flow from one part to another and provide an introduction that hooks your audience and then gives them a reason to stay engaged. If you want me to read a long article, attend a long meeting or listen to a long talk, then I will need to know what's in it for me, so tell me the benefits of paying attention right at the start.

Question and answer

What are the best ways to hook a listener or reader? They need to engage the brain and make your audience want to hear, see or read more. In some circumstances, a provocation can be very effective: for example, a provocative statement, undermining something familiar; a bold claim; or a challenge. Another common approach is to draw your audience in with the start of a story. You may finish it, to make a point that you will build on, or leave it hanging, to really grip your audience. One technique that you can use again and again throughout an article, a presentation or a film is a question. What happens when you pose your audience a question?

The brains of your audience members cannot help but try to find an answer and that is what you want: active brains. A good way to structure any communication is around a series of questions that your stakeholders will have. By doing this, you are being respectful of their natural curiosity and you are also directing the sequence of questions to suit the flow that you want to create. It also demonstrates your ethos: you have thought through the issues from their perspective, asking and answering the questions they would ask. This should sound like a familiar process.

Storytelling

Storytelling is a familiar process because that is what every culture has been doing since the start of recorded history. Stories establish a context and then create a situation which raises questions. If the reader, listener or viewer then cares enough to want an answer, you have them hooked. Humans are storytelling creatures and there is no better form for communicating compellingly. In their excellent book *Made to Stick*, authors Chip and Dan Heath identified six principles that make a message 'sticky', by which they mean 'understood and remembered, and having a lasting impact'. One of them is stories, but interestingly to me, stories can carry all of their other five principles:

1. *Simplicity* – because a story narrative can be kept simple and focused on what matters most.
2. *Unexpectedness* – because stories work well when there are surprises and reversals of fortune.
3. *Concreteness* – because stories provide a wealth of details and specific examples.
4. *Credibility* – because whilst stories do not have to be true, they resonate with their audience. Credibility lends ethos.
5. *Emotions* – because all good stories both deal with and conjure up strong emotions. Emotion lends pathos.

Persuasive

Messages are persuasive when they change the way people think in the ways that you intend. So the two important components of persuasive communication are, first, that people not only understand but that they also understand correctly what you are trying to get across and, second, that their perceptions, opinions or beliefs change. In the context of stakeholder communication, you want to be able to generate a greater measure of agreement with your point of view. We have already encountered the three essential factors in persuasive communication at the start of this chapter. As articulated by Aristotle, they are ethos, logos and pathos.

In classical rhetoric, which is still recognisable in many of today's political speeches and product advertising, this is the order that the persuader will use: first establishing their credibility and authority to be persuading you, then setting out the reasoning of their argument and, finally, providing an emotional reason why you should accept that argument. Persuaders know that few people make wholly logical decisions: most make an emotional decision, which they then 'rationalise' – justifying it with their own logic, which you may have helpfully provided for them.

My biggest mistake has been trying to rush a stakeholder into a decision with a bull-headed logical approach. First, your logical argument may not be theirs and, second, we don't always make a decision based on logic.

Let's examine ethos, logos and pathos in more depth.

Ethos

You establish your ethos by demonstrating that I can trust you. Consequently, I need to believe in your credibility, your integrity and character, and that you fully understand my concerns.

Fundamentally, your credibility rests upon your intellectual authority, but your stakeholders will make their assessments largely upon the confidence and clarity with which you speak and write. It is easy, as an expert, to use complex jargon that demonstrates the depth of your knowledge. However, true experts are able to put complicated ideas into simple terms, making it easy for everyone to understand. They understand where the boundary lies between simple and simplistic, and are able to use everyday language and appropriate metaphors to create clear and concise explanations.

Integrity is not negotiable for anyone who wants to make stakeholder engagement a professional discipline (see Appendix 5 on ethical stakeholder engagement). You can show your character through your honesty, your consistency of action and message, and in the restraint and emotional control that you show.

Perhaps the factor that has the most immediate impact on assessments of your ethos is your stakeholders' assessment of how you understand their needs and perceptions. They want you to show that their concerns are important to you – and hence the politicians' great urge to present themselves as men and women of the people, painting their electorate's concerns as their own concerns. In many cases, their pleas that this is the case ring hollow. When engaging with stakeholders, you need to be respectful, courteous, give them the time to put their thoughts to you and listen to them carefully.

Logos

You demonstrate your intellectual authority best when you can deploy a well-structured argument supported by strong evidence. The structure of a strong argument is simple at its core:

Step 1: Establish facts that both you and your stakeholders can agree on. These are sometimes referred to as 'commonplaces' and are beyond dispute. This starts the dialogue with agreement. It is easier to build agreement from agreement than from disagreement.

Step 2: Put your case, presenting the evidence in a logical sequence, focusing on two or three strong arguments at most. Ironically, more points will diminish the strength of your argument.

Step 3: Deal directly with arguments and counter-points that your stakeholders might make. If you can identify them in advance, you show that you have already taken them into account and this will weaken resistance.

Step 4: Now present a resolution between your case and the counter-arguments. Do so without directly refuting your stakeholder's points, which could easily cause conflict, but show how their points and yours can be reconciled with one another. One of the most useful techniques is the 'one more thing' gambit. Add one more fact into a conversation: 'You may not have been aware of this, but…' Now I don't need to change my mind and risk losing face; instead, I can say: 'Ahh, if I'd known that…'

Pathos

Most of our decisions are emotional, even though we often justify them with reason, and speakers using traditional approaches frequently end their speeches with an appeal to our emotions. This hammers home the conclusions that their logic compels.

This is why charitable appeals rarely press us with statistic after statistic to demonstrate the dreadfulness of, for example, children with cancer, without homes or with no access to clean water. Instead, they tell us about the life of one child, whose problems resonate with us as human beings, compelling us to compare their life with ours. Believing in the needs of this child is not enough to compel us to do something – we also need to care.

Two emotions dominate all others: desire and fear. Fear pushes us away from things, while desire pulls us towards things. In the short term, fear is the stronger of the two. Powerful advertising and political messages are often crafted to generate and exploit fear: fear of disease, poverty or danger, for example. In stakeholder communication, fear is often a good way to start people questioning long-held but unexamined beliefs or perceptions. Unfortunately, it is not a sustainable stakeholder engagement strategy and you would be wise, having generated some movement, to turn your attention to what your stakeholders desire, what they want and what is in it for them. Think about each stakeholder's own self-interest and speak or write in terms of the benefits to them using the evaluation you made using your stakeholder benefits matrix.

Fear of loss and desire to gain are two compelling motivators. Two others that we can use to build our persuasive force are curiosity and the need to build and maintain relationships. Fundamentally, we are learning creatures and social animals, and appeals to these drives can yield profound results.

Powerful

Powerful messages need to get the job done by being memorable and by encouraging your stakeholders to take action or make changes. Among the most important assets you have in creating powerful messages are the words you use. Some words seem to have more power to move people, whether spoken or written.

Not surprisingly, one of the most powerful words is 'you'. It addresses the listener or reader directly and attracts their attention. As is often the case, its power can be either positive or negative depending on the context and how you use it. So, for example, 'these are the benefits that you will get' has a positive impact, showing your stakeholder how you have personalised a list of benefits to what will matter to them. Alternatively, 'the problem is that you don't seem to realise what needs to happen' turns 'you' into a direct accusation that sets up conflict.

'Why' is another word that has great power to help or hinder your case. 'I am interested in why this software cannot provide us with the information we need' is the start of a purposeful investigation, yet 'I am interested in why you don't think this software can provide us with the information we need' is likely to be received as a direct challenge to the listener and evoke a defensive response. Notice that this latter example links 'why' with 'you'.

For persuaders, one word is particularly valuable: 'because'. When we hear the word, it flags up that there is a reason and prompts us to listen for it. In low-stakes situations, we even get lazy and don't listen to what the reason is: knowing there is one is enough to prompt a decision. However, for any serious stakeholder engagement, you will need to provide a good reason to justify your 'because'. This is the power of logos.

Tune in

Each of us has our own preferences about how we like to use language, which are probably linked to the way that we prefer to process information. Communication will always be at its most powerful when we speak or write in ways that mesh well with the other person's thought patterns.

Take, for example, the words 'mesh well' in the last sentence: they form a physical metaphor conjuring up gears. 'Mesh', 'gears' and 'to conjure up' are all 'kinaesthetic representations' that turn abstract ideas into solid, moving metaphors that evoke physical sensations. Some people use this kind of language a lot. Others don't see what they are getting at, because they prefer to view the world through the lens of 'visual representations'. Their language has more metaphors related to seeing than to doing. But if you want your language to chime with your whole audience, so that things sound right to everyone, you have to strike the right note for people who prefer 'auditory representations' and think in terms of their hearing sense. We all do all three of these, but most of us have a preference. Some people – mostly managers and technologists – become used to speaking in the sensory-free language of abstractions, preferring 'digital representations' rather than analogue representations. This makes it hard to form connections that resonate with audiences, who then fail to see the point clearly.

For an audience of stakeholders, use all types of language rather than defaulting to your own preferences. With one individual, listen to how they use language and skew your metaphors to match their preference.

There are other ways in which people think and if you can tune into them, you can hone your language to become still more powerful. Here are three examples:

- *Similarity and difference*: when you see two objects, or two ways of tackling a problem, do you first notice the similarities between them or is it the differences that strike you first? If I emphasise the right one, I will persuade you more powerfully.

- *Global or specific*: when you look at a problem or try to understand a new idea, do you zoom in on the details or pan out to the big picture as your way of making progress? If I choose the wrong focus, you will not feel that I am addressing your concerns.
- *Towards or away from*: if you think about your favourite food or your favourite hobbies, do you notice what draws you towards them – 'I like getting outside and being active' – or how they help you get away from what you don't like – 'I dislike sitting inside'? I need to spot the direction of your motivation and frame my arguments accordingly.

Tune into how people speak, spot what they say and get a feel for their speech patterns, because when you do, it will reveal a little about how they think. When you match your speech and writing patterns to theirs, your words, pictures or demonstrations will have more power.

Memory hooks

There are five hooks that you can use to help your stakeholders remember what you say or write based on what activates human memory:

1. *Primacy* – we tend to remember the first thing someone says or the first person we meet at a party, so put an important point right at the beginning.
2. *Frequency* – we tend to remember something we hear a lot or a person we keep bumping into, so re-state the important messages again and again.
3. *Recency* – we tend to remember the last thing someone says or the last person we meet at a conference, so reiterate an important point at the end.

So, tell them what you want them to remember, tell them it again and remind them what you have told them. There are two other ways to lock something into your stakeholders' memories:

4. *Novelty* – we tend to remember things that are unusual or emotionally charged, so deliver your message in a novel way. Unusual presentations, speeches or posters are often referred to as 'memorable' because we recognise this effect.
5. *Activity* – we tend to remember things that we get involved in. Activity forces information through several processing pathways in our brains, reinforcing memory: 'tell me and I will remember some; show me and

I will remember more; involve me and I will remember it all'. This is why we *engage* stakeholders rather than simply communicate with them.

Psychology

If you want your stakeholders to do something, then you need to understand the psychology behind action:

1. The first step is to avoid giving them too much choice. Choices inhibit action – when we fear we will make the wrong choice – so offer two or at most three choices at a time.
2. Be clear what you expect of them and then set a deadline. Most people are motivated by time pressure because it sets up fear of failure.
3. Alongside this, set up success points so that your stakeholders can also gain pleasure from a sense of progress once they get started.
4. Make the first success point particularly easy to achieve to create momentum and make starting less intimidating.
5. And, finally, set out a plan so that your stakeholders know what to expect and that their commitment is not open-ended. Ideally, articulate something like a five-point plan, but limit the number of steps to seven or fewer. If you think you need more, consolidate some, so that step four, for example, has three components. Long lists can be intimidating.

Sometimes you will want a stakeholder to change their mind. This is tricky and your first concern is to help them to avoid losing face, so avoid any blame for faulty perceptions – in fact, present their starting point as the logical one and then show them something they had not considered, such as a new fact or some unforeseen circumstances. And remember, your goal is the change of mind, not the credit, so be prepared to give your stakeholder the credit for your understanding: 'Something you said really got me thinking…'

There is a saying in some martial arts: 'move the mind – move the body'. It works both ways. Sometimes suggesting that a stakeholder takes a walk with you will quite literally help them to see an issue from a different point of view. If that doesn't work, encourage your stakeholder to assess a situation from someone else's perspective: 'How do you think Chris is feeling about this?'

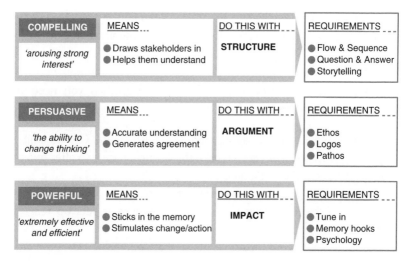

COMPELLING	MEANS ...	DO THIS WITH ...	REQUIREMENTS ...
'arousing strong interest'	● Draws stakeholders in ● Helps them understand	**STRUCTURE**	● Flow & Sequence ● Question & Answer ● Storytelling

PERSUASIVE	MEANS ...	DO THIS WITH ...	REQUIREMENTS ...
'the ability to change thinking'	● Accurate understanding ● Generates agreement	**ARGUMENT**	● Ethos ● Logos ● Pathos

POWERFUL	MEANS ...	DO THIS WITH ...	REQUIREMENTS ...
'extremely effective and efficient'	● Sticks in the memory ● Stimulates change/action	**IMPACT**	● Tune in ● Memory hooks ● Psychology

FIGURE 4.3 Compelling, persuasive and powerful communication

The figure above summarises the three concepts of compelling, persuasive and powerful.

Point of view

We cannot leave the topic of compelling, persuasive and powerful messages without addressing the topic of vision statements. Not only do most businesses, charities and publicly funded organisations now have a crisply worded vision statement, but, increasingly, so too do big change initiatives and projects. The problem with many of these vision statements is that they lack a real sense of vision.

A vision statement can be a powerful tool for engaging stakeholders as long as it spells out a vision that resonates strongly with them. This means that they need to understand it at a visceral as well as an intellectual level and it has to promise something that they really want. Here are five criteria for a powerful vision statement:

1. *Vision*: it must use imagery and concrete language. Vision statements that consist of abstract 'management-speak' not only lack vision, they are also uninspiring and unmemorable.
2. *Passion*: a good vision statement needs to create emotions and excitement – certainly a measure of desire, but maybe also a frisson of risk.

3. *Fit*: your vision statement must fit comfortably with the values and the culture of the people you have written it for, and it needs to work in the sense of pointing people towards the direction you want.

4. *Compelling*: your vision statement must also set a direction that the vast majority of your stakeholders want, otherwise they will not feel it to be compelling for them. It is OK if some stakeholders do not find it compelling; it is better to get it right for those who will want to follow than to make concessions for those who really want something else. But if too many stakeholders are alienated by the vision, then recognise that you are starting something new and that you need to ditch your old stakeholders and find new ones. This is sometimes the case when companies radically shift their product or service offerings, abandoning many old customers in search of a new market.

5. *Credible*: whatever your vision, it must be credible. This does not mean fully supported by detailed plans, but your vision must be rooted in reality and tied back to something tangible.

Delivering your message

Near the start of this chapter, we set out Stakeholder Rule Number 4: *communicate with people in the way that they like to communicate.*

This should be your guide in selecting which medium from among the vast array of possible delivery mechanisms you will use in engaging with each of your stakeholders. Appendix 4 presents a large list of formal and informal communication tools that are face to face, at a distance, written, online or broadcast.

There are so many choices that it pays to be creative. In large organisations, there is so much going on and so many initiatives underway that each must compete hard for our limited attention. Find ways to cut through this overload of information noise by innovating. A former colleague of mine was able to find a place and a time when people were not distracted by huge torrents of information and exploited it to create an information campaign for her project that she informally titled 'news in the loos'. This was, by the way, several years before advertising posters appeared in restaurant and service station toilets; if only she had patented the idea!

Rarely will one medium be enough. Select a portfolio, adopting the same principle as investors use: if you don't know that one approach is certain to work, adopt several, in the confident knowledge that while you cannot predict which will succeed, at least one is likely to.

Prioritisation and medium

One of the important factors to take into account will always be the level of investment and time that each medium demands. The gold standard for communication excellence will always be two people, face to face, communicating in the same language, in which they are both completely fluent. However, not only is this not always possible, but it is not always desirable. It is time-consuming, and this investment of time may not always be warranted by the message concerned or the importance of a stakeholder to your project. Other forms of communication will be a necessary part of your strategy.

The 'stakeholder pyramid' in Figure 4.4 below shows how you are likely to shift your engagement and communication strategy as you move from the few highly important stakeholders to the many lower-importance stakeholders. In the modern age, successful stakeholder engagement managers are making ever greater use of social media and web technologies, and these really do work well for many of them. Whilst at the top of the pyramid, direct one-to-one communication will doubtless

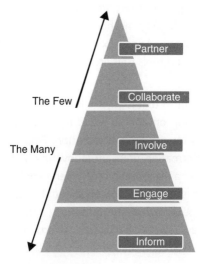

FIGURE 4.4 The stakeholder pyramid

remain your principal approach for your most vital stakeholders, even here, shared web spaces and secure, sophisticated online collaboration tools will be a part of your portfolio.

In Chapter 8, we will introduce additional tools that will help you to make an informed choice about which medium to use.

Crisis management

Stakeholder engagement will not always be carefully pre-planned. Sometimes things go wrong and you need to deal actively with a crisis. Your disaster or crisis plan needs to contain enough thinking, preparation and planning to allow you and your team to swiftly engage with your stakeholders constructively. Often this will be both directly and, when the crisis has a high profile, through the media.

Your crisis plan should designate a spokesperson, so, after the event, your first three steps will be: (1) to gather as much information about what has happened as quickly as possible; (2) to brief the spokesperson; and then (3) to start to consider the questions that the media and your stakeholders will most urgently want answers to, and prepare statements and responses accordingly.

You may also want to create a formal statement. This should be as open and comprehensive as possible, as well as scrupulously honest. Clearly you need to respect confidentiality, the due process of any potential investigations and the necessary fog of uncertainty, but any appearance of a cover-up or dissimulation will damage your reputation quickly. When communicating in times of stress and high emotion, always start with the big, significant facts first. People will struggle to assimilate details when emotions are running high. If you need to give instructions, do so clearly in plain language, breaking them into simple steps. Keep your message simple. This often means appointing a spokesperson who has a talent for this and, ideally, one who has had some training in this skill.

Identify your most important stakeholders at this time of crisis and, as much as possible, speak with them directly. These may be chief executives of organisations you do business with, political leaders or institutional shareholders. And don't forget your staff colleagues. They will often bear the brunt of dealing with the direct or consequential difficulties of your crisis. They need to feel re-assured that someone is in control and they need to know what to do and say. In relation to what your staff should say, compare these two sentences, which superficially have the same meaning:

- 'I don't know any more than you do'
  ... which makes me sound ill-informed.
- 'I am telling you everything that I know'
  ... which makes me sound open with regard to my information.

You will also need to ensure that you have authorised, social media-savvy people constantly reviewing what people are saying online, because questions may emerge that you need to respond to and you may have to take determined steps to protect your reputation.

If the crisis is a big one, consider appointing expert professional advisers quickly. While a good crisis communication consultant will be adept at building back reputations, you will save them a lot of work and yourself a lot of heartache and fees if you minimise damage from the outset by taking expert advice as soon as possible.

EXAMPLES OF PROGRAMME CRISES

Failure of prototype, pilot or test

Put this into a clear context: this is what prototypes, pilots and tests are designed for – to allow us to fail safely so that we can learn and avoid the failure of the final system. Show determination to learn and use the experience well, and set out a timescale for the next steps, going no further than you can genuinely foresee.

Financial problems

Get the information out in a timely manner to prevent rumour overtaking you. Set out a clear process for understanding and addressing the situation, and consider appointing an external reviewer or adviser to get to the bottom of the problem. Make it clear that you will release substantive information as soon as you are able to without breaching financial regulations, but be equally clear that you will not be giving day-by-day briefing. If you can, speak with individuals or small groups to let them know how they may or will be affected. People will be more comforted by an honest assessment of possible outcomes accompanied by 'we don't know yet which will happen' than by a period of silence or by vague re-assurance.

Natural disasters

Put your focus on hard information and what people need to do. Become an authoritative source of information and instruction and then, as the situation stabilises and you have gained people's trust, move your communication to focus on recovery. Consistency is vital and, whilst you must remain scrupulously honest, set aside any discussion of blame or even the cause of the crisis until the situation is stable and rescue activities are concluded.

Product recall or service failure

Start by assessing how the presentation of your message will need to differ between the customers or service users who are directly affected and other stakeholders, whose perceptions will be shaped by what you communicate and how you get your message out. Also be mindful of any safety concerns and therefore the urgency and directness of your message. Thinking more about the long-term impact on your reputation than about the immediate fall-out will probably guide you towards doing the right thing. Clear instructions about what products are affected and how to act are essential. Think about your whole supply chain and consider having your most senior executive issue an apology quickly – the chances are that they will be called upon to do so eventually, so why not get ahead of the pressure?

Regulatory or legal investigation

Announce the published scope of the investigation and declare your intention to cooperate fully. Welcome the light that it will cast on failings and emphasise your willingness to learn from the process and findings so as to strengthen the integrity of what you are doing. As soon as possible, announce who will act as primary liaison with investigators and choose someone with the seniority and independence that reinforces your message.

Sudden loss of senior sponsor or change leader

Your primary concern is to demonstrate continuity and control: 'the king is dead, long live the king'. A successor may not be evident, but quickly announce a temporary leader who will have a clear remit to maintain stability and progress. The announcement should be made quickly to avoid rumour and speculation, and by someone very senior so as to show that the issue has the attention of those at the very top of the organisation.

WISE WORDS FROM REAL PRACTITIONERS

Data – and how you use it – is an important aspect of stakeholder engagement. Clear visibility of key statistics within the shared office space, with near-real-time updates ensures stakeholders can see what progress you are making. It is more important to use data than to wait until it is 100 per cent accurate. As you start to use it, people will let you know of corrections – this more quickly builds an accurate date set and allows productivity without a long delay. Look for good enough rather than perfect – then you can get on with delivering!

5
Gentle Persuasion: Soft Power

Gentle persuasion often achieves more than stronger tactics ever can and it is fundamentally based on liking. We do more for the people we like than for those we either don't know or don't like. So what is the secret to being liked? Let's ask a selection of people to get some typical answers:

'I like people I trust'
– so practice openness and integrity so that people feel they can trust you.

'I like people I see often'
– this may be a case of the chicken and the egg, but increase the frequency of meetings.

'I like people I can believe'
– so demonstrate your credibility and depth of knowledge and experience.

'I like people who listen to me'
– so take time to focus on people and what they are saying.

'I like people who help out'
– so offer practical assistance.

'I like people who respect me'
– so don't enforce unwanted assistance.

'I like people who are like me'
– so demonstrate how our interests and perspectives overlap.

'I like people who are like I want to be'
– so set high standards and a good example without bragging or arrogance.

'I like people whom the people I like like'
– so associate with the people I like, trust and respect.

'I like people who make me feel good'
– so smile, offer sincere praise and show me that you respect me.

None of this is about appealing to authority and little of it even relies on the strength of your argument or communication skills. Soft power is all about the ability to persuade by creating a personality that people want to follow. It is influence exclusively through social relationships.

In the context of stakeholder engagement, 'social influence' is by far the most important corner of a triad of three forms of influence: social, economic and status.

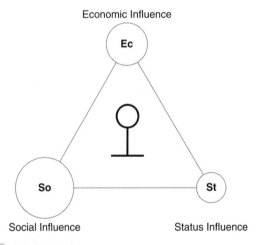

Economic Influence

Social Influence   Status Influence

FIGURE 5.1 / **Triad of influence**

We achieve social influence with our personality and through the relationships we form with other people. One of the consequences of the massive rise of social media is the massive amplification this achieves, not simply through our ability to reach more people, but also through the immediacy of their social influence amplifying our own. A well-thought-out social media campaign can deliver big stakeholder engagement results.

'Economic influence' refers to the impact of exchange of goods, services, favours, concessions or promises. This creates a sense of obligation that the persuader can call upon to create the influence they need. The obligation – and therefore the influence – arises because of a deeply felt need in most of us to reciprocate actions, to bring our relationships into what we perceive as a fair balance. We feel uncomfortable with inequity and therefore act to restore equity. Economic influence thus arises as a result of making people feel uncomfortable. We are literally buying our influence and so this does not fit well with a desire for open engagement with our stakeholders.

'Status influence' is even more asymmetric than economic influence because the message is that you cannot balance the mismatch between your status and mine by your actions, yet you are constrained in some way to comply with my wishes. The status imbalance may relate to power, knowledge, experience and, depending on the culture, demographic factors like age, gender and even ethnicity. Immediately, it should be clear how distasteful this form of influence can be, and status influence must therefore be a last refuge of someone lacking any other mechanism for persuading stakeholders.

Of course, we all deploy all three forms of influence and my total influence over you is the cumulative effect of all three. This chapter, however, is about social influence.

What is soft power?

The term 'soft power' was coined by Joseph S. Nye in his 1990 book *Bound to Lead: The Changing Nature of American Power*. He later refined the concept in his 2004 book *Soft Power: The Means to Success in World Politics*. You can see from this that I have appropriated his term for our purposes: Nye is an expert in geopolitics and national security. He contrasted soft power with hard power and economic power; the coercion of military force and economic sanctions or incentives, respectively. The three, he suggested, should be deployed together, with soft power offering exceptional value for money. He asserted that: 'Seduction is always more effective than coercion.' This is the long-term strategy behind the UK's foreign policy, which has historically focused on diplomacy, relatively high levels of aid and assistance, support for reconstruction and infrastructure development, and media interventions, of which the BBC World Service is globally pre-eminent. Other soft power initiatives used by the UK include cultural exchanges (the British Council), international volunteering (Voluntary Service Overseas – VSO) and student exchange opportunities.

Soft power in stakeholder engagement

What are the equivalents of these initiatives in your stakeholder engagement context? Each of them fulfils one or more imperatives on the global stage: demonstrating cultural norms that others may share or aspire to, conforming to a set of political values that others may share or aspire to, and delivering benign policies that are designed to aid and assist in people's lives. You can do all of these within your own project or programme of change:

- Engage openly and encourage a balanced dialogue where listening and bridge-building are prioritised over telling and compelling.
- Ensure that your initiative provides valuable benefits to your stakeholders, possibly investing in additional benefits, beyond the core requirements.
- Provide honest and reliable communications that people prefer to use as their primary information source.
- Let stakeholders get actively involved in aspects of the project and encourage members of your team to shadow stakeholders to find out first-hand what their challenges are like, to understand their challenges and how they shape their perceptions.
- Practise the highest standards of governance and self-regulation.

Soft power is part of an environment of influence

Each of us is influenced by many factors, which create competing pressures on us. These can be characterised as follows:

Personal   The influence of close or charismatic individuals, or small, well-defined groups with coherent aims.

Local   The influence of the groups of people in close proximity to us. These may have little coherence.

Cultural   The influence of a large accumulation of people averages out differences and renders extreme perceptions impotent (unless extremism becomes the prevailing culture). Soft power aims to create a coherent source of cultural influence.

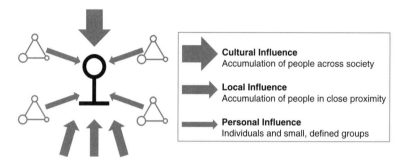

FIGURE 5.2 / The environment of influence

The three purposes of soft power

You are not concerned with geopolitics, but with people who are stakeholders in a significant change in your organisation or community. Therefore, your three objectives will be more modest in their scope, though very much the same in their principles. We use soft power to:

1. shape our stakeholders' perceptions and opinions;
2. reinforce supportive perceptions and opinions;
3. shift critical perceptions and opinions.

/ Deploying soft power

In this section, we will look at four approaches to using soft power to achieve these ends:

1. *Reputation*: how stakeholders perceive you is critical to your soft power.
2. *Attraction*: Nye's definition of soft power places attraction at its heart.
3. *Motivation*: creating a drive for stakeholders to act on their perceptions and opinions.
4. *Relationships*: a trusting relationship is the long-term goal of a soft power strategy.

Reputation

Many things contribute to the way people think of you, and integrity is central to this. All of the other things, like how nice, helpful, insightful or supportive you are, rest on this central plank. You know this of course, because reputation is a big part of our social functioning and we grow up with the concept and the reality, whatever culture we are in.

In Shakespeare's *Othello*, Iago is both cynical and elegiac about reputation – marking the character's duplicity. In Act 2, Scene 3, he says:

> Reputation is an idle and most false imposition; oft got without merit, and lost without deserving.

While later, in Act 3, Scene 3, he also says:

> But he that filches from me my good name
> Robs me of that which not enriches him
> And makes me poor indeed.

We know that reputation is something we build with care, but that we can lose in an instant. It starts with your personal conduct and the way you treat people. When you are in a hurry, or if you are angry, it is easy to fall into a disrespectful way of dealing with people, which says 'I am focused on me and the way I feel'. Ironically, brusqueness and anger almost never get the best from a situation.

A simple exercise is to think about the people you most respect for being able to achieve the sort of things you want to achieve and to write down what they have a reputation for. Where there is considerable overlap, you will have a template for the reputation you may want to build for yourself. But take care over the integrity component – a hot topic in business leadership and management in recent years has been authenticity. Choose to build a reputation that is authentic to who you really are at your core.

As your reputation grows, if it is authentic to you, so will your confidence in yourself, which will enhance the way you come across to people. If you are confident in who you are, this will often come across as charisma, the ability to inspire enthusiasm in others.

As well as your demeanour, what you know and what you do will be significant factors in building and maintaining your reputation. This means investing constantly in your skills and expertise, staying up-to-date with the latest knowledge and thinking in your chosen areas of specialism. Some professions have a requirement for regular continuing professional development, and in these, professional reputation is enhanced not by staying up-to-date, but by becoming deeply expert or creating original ideas or interpretations.

People do say that actions speak louder than words, and in the arena of reputation-building, this is undoubtedly true. Henry Ford got it right when he said: 'You can't build a reputation on what you are going to do.'

Many readers will know of people whose reputation is built upon a single influential act early in their careers. Many will also know someone who has spent a whole career trying to shed an equally powerful adverse reputation gained in their younger days.

BEING BELIEVED

Is your reputation so strong that people would not for a moment doubt your words? It may be, but it does no harm to remember how to present an argument or respond to questions in a way that will enhance your believability. All of these tips echo what makes a good reputation, but are presented here as ways to deal with a particular event:

- Listen carefully and then pause before making your point. This shows you to be courteous and thoughtful. Be scrupulously polite, without being mannered or, worse, submissive.

- Choose clothing and grooming that your stakeholders will recognise as respectful and appropriate. Looks should not matter, but the fact is that they often do.

- Separate facts from opinions and choose which are appropriate to the circumstances.

- Slow your speech down to ensure it is clear and deliberate, giving the impression of confidence in what you are saying.

- Keep entirely to the point and avoid answering questions that have not been asked. This will look evasive, no matter how helpful you are trying to be. For the same reason, keep your comments simple and in plain language.

- Avoid extra words that weaken your message, like truly, honestly, really or I'm sure. Perhaps even worse is hyperbole – exaggerating for effect. If numbers are big, quote the actual number and give an appropriate comparison.
- When you have made your point or given your answer, stop.

Attraction

The strongest ways we create attraction are familiarity, similarity and charm. Unless you do something to upset me, the longer and more closely I feel I know you, the more I will probably come to like you. So the first tip in creating soft power through attraction is to get to know your stakeholders and continuously reinforce your relationship with regular meetings. Leil Lowndes is an author and coach who never talks in terms of stakeholders, yet her books are filled with valuable tips and advice. In *How to Talk to Anyone: 92 Little Tricks for Big Success in Relationships*, she offers one of her best, which will jump-start the process of familiarity. She calls it the 'Hello Old Friend' technique and all you need to do, just before meeting somebody, is to imagine them to be a long-lost friend whom you have wanted to meet again for years. This will translate into your body language and communicate that you value the other person tremendously, adding a positive charge to the start of your meeting.

We also seem more familiar and more similar when we share aspects of each other's attitudes, so use your second position analysis (page 50) to help you understand how they see the world. This will help with building rapport, but there are a lot of other ways you can use similarity to build a rapport, from adopting similar dress codes to using similar words and phrases. At its simplest, however, common interests establish similarity so effectively that finding them is often the first thing we do when we meet someone new: 'Where are you from? What line of work are you in? Do you know anyone here?' All of these questions are designed to find something you have in common. An old sales trick is to remember to talk about FROGS at the start of a meeting with a customer or prospect:

- Friends in common.
- Relationships and family.

- Organisations.
- Geography.
- Social and recreation – or, with some people; sport.

Charm is shockingly effective: it is astonishing how far a genuine smile and sincere praise will take you in becoming liked by people. Listening well is also a highly valued trait because it is so rare in much of our modern society. When you commit to paying close attention to what your stakeholders say, they will really appreciate it and, given enough time to talk with nothing more than gently prompting questions and calm affirmations, they will often discover a change imperative or a solution for themselves. Listening gives you a way to talk someone round to your way of thinking without having to argue with them. The secret to good listening is to turn off the voice in your head, which usually fills in gaps with your own thoughts and comments inwardly on what you are hearing. Instead, become aware of your listening and quite deliberately focus on paying close attention to the other person. When you do this, you will almost certainly have to leave a pause when they stop talking before you are ready to ask your next question. That is good: it signals that what they have just told you is valuable and not obvious, so your brief silence will come across as respectful.

CASE STUDY

As a more junior practitioner, it feels as if stakeholder engagement is focused on yourself and impressing stakeholders with what you do and say. From the perspective of experience, it is about saying less and listening more, and about asking good questions to help clarify what the stakeholder is really trying to articulate. Effective engagement does not mean having all the answers for everyone; it is about establishing effective working relationships to build up the trust that is necessary to work through to the answers. This means good listening and good questioning.

The practitioner, a senior change and programme management executive, was attending a project board meeting for the first time, and directors were getting very frustrated with the project manager. He was answering questions quickly, without carefully listening to them or reading the room. The experienced practitioner was able to create a strong positive impact very quickly simply by asking a few well-chosen clarifying questions that helped everyone get to the bottom of the issues.

Listening is not the same as hearing. Really listening takes effort and yields results in understanding and rapport-building. Always listen with your eyes as well as your ears. Body language will give you strong clues as to mood and intensity – and sometimes missing information.

Finally, one of the most powerful words you can use is my name. Each of us enjoys having our name remembered and used correctly. By correctly, I mean pronounced as we pronounce it ourselves and not over-used. Some shop assistants have a habit – probably due to poor training – of over-using a customer's name; this can be very annoying. Make a habit of remembering people's names. For the many readers who are thinking that this is a step too far and much too difficult, here is a little secret: the commonest reason why people forget names is because when they are introduced to someone, they don't care enough what the name is. So they don't pay attention to it – it goes in one ear, passes through the brain without registering and then out of the other. Now they are ready to move on to the next person without having paid the first person the respect of caring what they are called.

So notice a name when it is given to you. Pay attention and then repeat it back to check pronunciation. If the spelling is tricky or if there is more than one possible spelling, you have a perfectly legitimate reason to make more of the name, helping you to lock it in: 'Is that Stuart with a "u" or Stewart with a "w"?' Another way to help lock the name in is to ask about it; its country or culture of origin or its meaning, for example. Now use the name – sparingly – during your conversation and, as you do, try to find a mental link to help make the name stick. When you use the name, use it as the person introduced it: don't turn a Mike into Michael or Katherine into Kate. These are overly familiar at best and can cause offence at worst. When you link it in your mind, however, the more outrageous the connections you can form, the more memorable they will be: 'Kim, with the big ears, like an elephant, which Kipling's Kim rode' – in your mind, remember, not out loud! Finally, when you say goodbye, use the name and, if you have any doubts that you will remember it as they leave, get your notebook out and make a note.

Call sheets and call logs

There is little that frustrates people more than leaving a phone message and then finding the person does not have the courtesy to get back to them – or is it just me? I don't think it is just me, so make sure you are scrupulous about returning calls. Many professional communicators who rely on the phone as a significant part of their work use call sheets to record incoming calls and messages that they need to respond to. Either an assistant records the calls or they themselves compile them from voicemail, answerphone, text and email messages that need a response. The template below illustrates what a typical call sheet looks like.

Template 5.1   Inbound call sheet

Call sheet for:				Date:	
Time	*Caller*	*Affiliation*	*Number*	*Message/Subject*	☑

You can download a sample call sheet template from www.theinfluence agenda.co.uk.

If you are taking messages for someone, be fastidious in getting the relevant details correct: read back the contact number, spell out the name and write the message down in full. More than one project has suffered a serious setback due to messages going astray or being relayed inaccurately.

Equally important is that you record your phone conversations, both inbound and outbound. The best approach is a daybook – a notebook into which you record everything. At the start of a call, write the date and time, and the name and affiliation of the person you are speaking with, and record any important comments. This creates what is called a 'contemporaneous record' of the call and, in a legal dispute, it is a valuable piece of evidence of what transpired. Disputes aside, this is your day-to-day record and will help you avoid losing valuable information. Once a day, review your daybook, create action lists for the coming day and formally file important notes for your team to be able to access.

Some people prefer call logs or call record sheets. You can download sample call log or call record sheet templates from www.theinfluenceagenda.co.uk.

Motivation

There are four types of motivation and you can deploy soft power to provide two of them to motivate stakeholders.

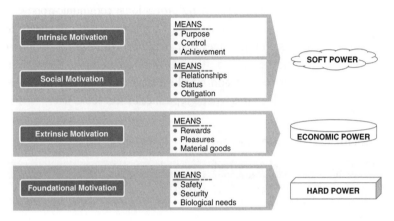

FIGURE 5.3   Motivation and power

'Foundational motivators' include things like safety, security and biological needs, and it is hard power that primarily assures or threatens these. 'Extrinsic motivators' come from outside of ourselves and include things like material possessions, pleasures and rewards. These are provided through the use of economic power.

It is 'social motivators' and 'intrinsic motivators' that can be met through the use of soft power.

Social motivators

Social motivators include the need for relationships with other people and status among those people – perhaps even power. Here we also find our desire to create a good reputation, which we discussed earlier in this section. The other important area of social motivation – that is met less well by soft power – is obligation or a sense of duty. However, we can regard this as a need to reciprocate favours done or status granted, so whilst on the face of it, this is met by economic power, the use of soft power can generate a sense of obligation that is one of the main reasons why nations deploy it geopolitically.

Within an organisation, social motivations arise at different levels and you must understand which one to appeal to for each stakeholder. With a diverse group, you will need to appeal to all five of the below:

1. *Society* – some stakeholders are motivated by their need to feel part of society, their desire to contribute to it or even their sense of duty towards it. Patriotism is an example of the latter.
2. *Customers and clients* – in some organisations, dedication to clients goes beyond what the organisation promotes to drive good service, to a calling or vocation. The not-for-profit and caring sectors are filled with people motivated like this.
3. *The organisation and its shareholders or members* – Etzioni (see page 18) showed us three sources of power that organisations have. Normative power, the ability to secure compliance through shared beliefs and values, motivates stakeholders in the organisation to commit themselves to its objectives.
4. *Immediate colleagues* – as social beings, we experience a powerful urge to relate to, support and achieve status among our working groups and teams.
5. *Me* – at times, some people's primary motivation is to look after themselves and ask 'what's in it for me?' This is not necessarily anti-social; more likely, it suggests a perceived need to fulfil one or more of the needs represented by the foundational motivators.

Intrinsic motivators

Intrinsic motivators are, ultimately, the most satisfying. They are the subject of much contemporary research in the field, as well as popular management books, like Daniel Pink's influential *Drive*. These include our need for purpose and meaning, which accounts for the most common question asked by stakeholders (whether they articulate it or not): 'Why?' If you don't answer the 'why?' question, then resistance is sure to follow.

Another intrinsic motivator is the need for control in our lives. By engaging respectfully with your stakeholders, you can provide them with the control they need. This is vitally important: the need for control is so strong in us that, when deprived of it, we seek exhaustively to re-assert it. If we cannot control what we expect to control, we will seize control of a situation in any way that we can, which, if there is no other route open to us, means active resistance. A powerful response to stakeholders who oppose or are sceptical about a change is to involve them and give them real control in one area of the programme where their influence is legitimate. This gives an outlet to the need for control.

The need for control is linked to our need for certainty – control allows us to generate it. So, another way that you can mitigate a stakeholder's impulse to take control is to demonstrate that they can have confidence in the future and do not need to exert their control. But beware: too much certainty leaves us feeling bored, stifled and not in control. We also need a measure of stimulation from variety and surprise. Creating an element of excitement in your project through pilots and participation can also be a valuable way to engage stakeholders and meet their need for control.

The third area of intrinsic motivation is the desire for worthwhile achievements that give us a sense of developing ourselves and growing in terms of our skill level and expertise. This area is ripe for engaging some of your stakeholders by offering them opportunities to contribute and participate in your project's successes.

Relationships

A trusting relationship is the long-term goal of a soft power strategy. There are two stages in building long-term relationships: forming and maintaining the relationship.

Forming a relationship with a stakeholder

Nothing builds a relationship better than meeting face to face, but, whether or not you are able to do this, is there a way to accelerate the creation of trust between you and your stakeholder? It turns out that there is – it is a process called 'swift trust'.

This concept was first developed by Debra Meyerson, Karl Weick and Roderick Kramer, and is the subject of a chapter in the cross-disciplinary review book *Trust in Organizations* edited by Kramer and Tom Tyler. In some circumstances, trust can be built quickly within a team and the authors identify six helpful steps to take. These can easily be adapted to your stakeholder engagement process:

1. *Presuming each team member has earned their place*
   Approach each stakeholder with the attitude that they deserve the right to be involved in some way with your project, that their views

matter and that you will respect their experiences and perceptions as being relevant.

2. *Trusting other people's expertise and knowledge*
   No adaptation is needed; where your stakeholder has relevant expertise and knowledge, trust it.

3. *Creating shared goals and a shared recognition or reward scheme*
   Identifying common goals is a vital step. Using your benefits register (page 89), you can also show how the changes bring rewards for your stakeholder as well as for you.

4. *Defining a clear role for each person to play*
   Part of your stakeholder engagement strategy must be about the role that each stakeholder will play either in your project or in the consultation or promotion process.

5. *Focusing on tasks and actions*
   Keeping a relationship transactional in its early stages allows each party to focus on results and then evaluate each other through working together. With a few small successes under your belt, trust will follow quickly.

6. *Taking responsibility and acting responsively*
   I hope that, by this stage in the book, these should go without saying. Take responsibility for engaging and for any commitments you make to your stakeholders. And respond quickly and efficiently to their concerns, requests, advice and other interventions. This does not mean agreeing with them or doing as they ask, but if you are not going to, acknowledge their contribution courteously and let them know your reasons for declining.

Swift trust emerges when people are willing to suspend their doubts and concerns about colleagues and just get on with a shared task. They focus on their goals, their roles and the time constraints they are under.

WISE WORDS FROM REAL PRACTITIONERS

Prepare for conversations carefully – especially when you only have three minutes with the CEO or some other high-power stakeholder. Make sure you identify your end-game (what you want to achieve) and your minimum reasonable acceptable outcome from the meeting.

Maintaining a relationship with a stakeholder

Once you have built your relationships, you have done the difficult part – now for the hard part ... hard work, that is. You have made a big investment, so it would be foolish to let the relationship decay. And it will do so if you fail to work at it.

Aside from regular contact, which can use any medium, you can gradually build the strength of the relationship with occasional help and assistance or by doing small favours. One of the simplest professional or business favours is to send copies of, or links to, articles your contacts may find interesting, with a simple message that when you read it, you thought of them. This does four things: it emphasises that you think of them, shows you know what is interesting to them, demonstrates your generosity in making the time to follow up and, finally, subtly hints that you read widely and keep up-to-date, thereby emphasising your technical and intellectual authority. Whatever favours you exchange, be careful about their scale; the very last thing you want is for your favour to be perceived as an inappropriate inducement. Sharing information like this has no monetary value.

Some of your strongest relationships will be with your core allies. These are easy to neglect when the pressures of dealing with urgent matters and disruptive stakeholders seem to take up all of your time. Never let this happen: time invested in maintaining these relationships will nearly always pay off. Token emails are not enough: treat them like a cross between royalty and a counsellor, and they will look for ways that they can help you with your troubles.

As your relationship with a stakeholder grows stronger, true, deep collaboration becomes a possibility, offering a way for both of you to enhance your outcomes from the project. It takes a lot of work to make collaboration effective, so only consider this move if the potential benefits outweigh the amount of time and effort it will take. In particular, there is unlikely to be a complete overlap between your interests and goals, in your resources and power bases, and, with a stakeholder organisation, in your cultures. These may, however, be the reasons to collaborate, to bring interests and even cultures closer together, and to access each other's resources and sources of power.

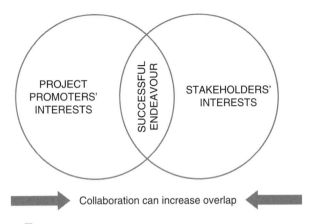

Collaboration can increase overlap

FIGURE 5.4 / **Collaboration**

Conflict

The biggest challenge you will face in any relationship will be conflict. The process for resolving it is conceptually simple: the challenge is in persevering and making it work, often in the face of high emotional intensity. The steps involved are as follows:

1. Decide that you are going to manage your emotions, set the feelings of anger or hurt aside and make the choice to engage positively, putting progress ahead of pride.
2. Arrange a meeting with your stakeholder in a suitable neutral place, framing it as being about rebuilding the relationship and working together to resolve your differences.
3. Show your appreciation for the courage your stakeholder is showing in engaging in resolution.
4. Listen to your stakeholder's point of view and share yours, making sure that facts, feelings and concerns emerge. The tougher the messages, the harder you will need to listen and the more you need to show respect for what you hear. Show that you understand their position and demonstrate empathy for the way they feel.
5. Set out what you each require from the situation and work together to agree the criteria for a worthwhile resolution to the issue. If you establish that you have mutually incompatible objectives that cannot

overlap, you can agree to disagree on cordial, even if not friendly, terms.

6. Now explore options for ways to achieve your outcomes and resolve your differences. Focus on actions and jointly prioritise what you will do. Be generous with credit for good ideas, putting resolution ahead of recognition.

7. Close the process with an agreement about what steps comprise the resolution and your respective commitments about what you will do.

Exerting gentle persuasion

If you want to influence someone's behaviour, you must first understand what drives their behaviour. Sometimes it is a reflex reaction to circumstances, so unless you control those circumstances, their behaviour is out of your (and their) control. At other times, their behaviour is planned and that allows you to influence it. Icek Ajzen is Professor of Psychology at the University of Massachusetts who has studied this extensively and developed a 'Theory of Planned Behaviour' (see his 1991 article 'The Theory of Planned Behavior', *Organisational Behavior and Human Decision Processes*, 50: 179–211).

The Theory of Planned Behaviour suggests that our behaviour is driven by 'behavioural intentions', which are themselves determined by three things:

1. *Our attitude towards the behaviour*
   To form this, we consider each of the likely consequences of the behaviour and factor in our beliefs about how likely they are (their expectancy).
   If you want to change my behaviour, change my assessment of consequences or likelihoods.
2. *Our subjective assessment of societal norms about the behaviour*
   This is based on an aggregate of all our beliefs about how society works.
   If you want to change my behaviour, help me relate it to social norms.
3. *Our perceptions of factors that might control our behaviour*
   This is a subjective estimate of how much control we have over our performance of the behaviour.
   If you want to change my behaviour, show me how I can control my actions to get the results I want.

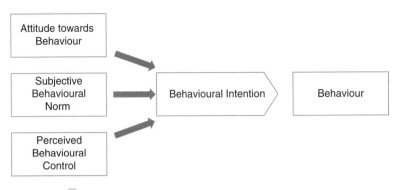

FIGURE 5.5 / **Theory of Planned Behaviour**

This model is used by professional influencers, like those in the advertising industry. It explains, for example, why information alone rarely results in behaviour change: Ajzen found information not to be a major factor in driving intention, except to the extent that it modifies one of the three factors above. This model is also valuable to change agents who want to influence behavioural change.

Adapting your approach to your stakeholder's style

It should go without saying that you will need to adjust your approach to stakeholder engagement to accommodate the personality and style of each stakeholder. There are a lot of models of personality, but one of the most useful is David Merrill and Roger Reid's 'Social Styles' model detailed in their book *Personal Styles & Effective Performance*. This is particularly useful because it makes no pretence at delving into underlying psychology, but instead focuses on the personality that is on show. The authors chose not to concern themselves with why we appear as we do. The model categorises the ways people behave in social situations, according to two broad characteristics: 'assertiveness' and 'responsiveness'.

Merrill and Reid use these terms in very specific ways that differ somewhat from their day-to-day usages. They used 'assertiveness' to mean the way people prefer to get what they want, ranging from a low-assertiveness style, which prefers to ask, to a high-assertiveness style, which prefers to tell. The responsiveness scale measures the extent to which we allow our emotions to show, from a highly responsive 'emoting' style to a low-responsiveness 'controlling' style. These give rise to four social styles, as illustrated in Figure 5.6 below.

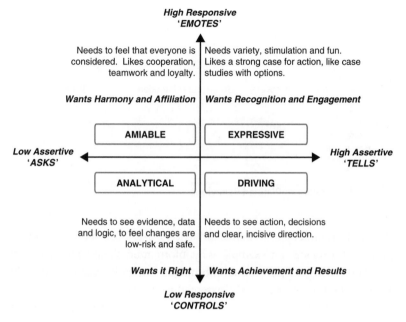

**High Responsive
'EMOTES'**

Needs to feel that everyone is considered. Likes cooperation, teamwork and loyalty. | Needs variety, stimulation and fun. Likes a strong case for action, like case studies with options.

Wants Harmony and Affiliation | *Wants Recognition and Engagement*

AMIABLE | EXPRESSIVE

**Low Assertive
'ASKS'** | **High Assertive
'TELLS'**

ANALYTICAL | DRIVING

Needs to see evidence, data and logic, to feel changes are low-risk and safe. | Needs to see action, decisions and clear, incisive direction.

Wants it Right | *Wants Achievement and Results*

**Low Responsive
'CONTROLS'**

FIGURE 5.6 / Social styles

The analytical social style

The analytical stakeholder wants things to be right, so you need to show them evidence and data, using rigorous reasoning in drawing your conclusions. They also like to see plans and will happily immerse themselves in details. They tend to be cautious and risk averse, so emphasise factors like reliability, safety and security.

The amiable social style

The amiable stakeholder cares more about people and how they are feeling. They want to feel that everyone's needs and wishes are being considered and want to be involved in a team endeavour. They will avoid confrontation and so can appear to other social styles to be evasive.

The expressive social style

The expressive stakeholder wants to be fully involved and to get recognition for their contribution. They are intellectual moths, attracted to bright lights and then moving on, and so need constant stimulation. For them, a persuasive case needs examples and options. They are highly energetic and enthusiastic, so, if you don't harness this, someone else may do so.

The driving social style

The driving stakeholder wants to be in charge. Of most importance for them is results, so they need to see clear action and real progress. Involve them in decisions or they will fight you, and ensure that they see clear incisive direction. Details can bore them, so start with the big picture and focus in until they tell you to stop.

Tactics and strategies

The time has come to offer you some specific tactics and strategies for deploying soft power.

The simple things matter

Make yourself as easy to deal with as you can. If you are successful, stakeholders will want to engage with you, so prioritise the simple things like appearance, courtesy, listening, keeping your promises, meeting your commitments and being on time. Make your stakeholders feel important and keep them all informed; surprises can undermine a relationship quickly and permanently. Know when to stop and back off, and get good at saying 'I don't know' and admitting when you are wrong. The reality is you often won't know and you will sometimes be wrong. There is nothing wrong with either of these as long as you handle the situation well. Remain optimistic yet realistic and always offer your stakeholders a choice.

The three levers for changing minds

There are three principal ways to change someone's mind:

1. *Cognitive*
   The hardest is to use the facts and do so well. People often don't make choices on the evidence – they choose the evidence to support their choices. Build the evidence to support the right choice from evidence and reason.
2. *Representational*
   This is what gets in the way of cognitive persuasion – how we understand the ideas and information we receive. This is affected by things like prior experiences, selective hearing and existing beliefs.

Real-world events can also colour our judgements by providing highly compelling experiences that shift our priorities.

3. *Emotional*

Our emotional state (what psychologists call 'affect') will not only influence our representations, it will also dictate what 'feels right'. Most judgements are made from an emotional perspective, so you must appeal to stakeholders' feelings as much as their minds.

The power of words

In Chapter 4 (pages 100–101), we saw that the words 'you', 'why' and 'because' are particularly powerful. So too is the word 'we'. 'We' engages a sense of collegiality between the speaker and the listener, so use it liberally when you are working with a stakeholder.

Questions also have a lot of power, because of what happens when you ask one. In their heads, your listeners or readers are thinking what the answer may be. Not only does this engage their attention, but if you ask the right question in the right way, they will get the right answer. Now that answer is theirs, not yours. This means you don't have to do any persuading at all.

The ultimate in using words to persuade – sophistry aside – is storytelling. Stories persuade gently because they create a real world in the mind of the listener or reader. Your stakeholder may not trust you, but they trust themselves and if the story has a reality to them, then the storyteller fades into the background. In addition, stories allow the storyteller to control perceptions, are more memorable than facts and, because of their emotional content, can address all three levers for changing minds: cognitive, representational and emotional.

Pilots and prototypes

Pilots and prototypes allow stakeholders to get their hands on the future. Nothing engages more than a chance to play, and the trial provides the perfect platform for gathering opinions, challenging prejudices and testing perceptions. Most project managers like pilots and prototypes for their ability to deliver data and mitigate risk, but a stakeholder engagement manager will know that they are a vital strategy that can provide support to their supporters and can provide evidence that detractors may have been wrong up to now.

Borrowed influence

Any apex stakeholders who conspicuously support the change you are leading can provide powerful endorsement in your campaign of gentle persuasion. They will be masters of attraction and motivation with a strongly positive reputation and excellent relationships: this is almost a definition of an apex stakeholder. Ask them to speak for you and get permission to use their name in saying things like 'I understand that Sidney feels that...' or 'Nitan clearly favours...'.

Constructive conflict

Here are two dangerous tactics to be used with great care. Both create conflict with a stakeholder.

If a stakeholder is constantly complaining, but you assess their impact to be low and their resolve to be weak, you can give them a simple ultimatum by asking: 'What are we going to do about it?' The 'we', you will notice, forces them to share responsibility. If they have a good answer, you have shifted their position and have a good result. If they come up with nothing, you have undermined their credibility. If you want to take an even bigger risk (with a potentially higher upside or worse downside), do this in public. The downside will be if they bear a grudge and subsequently gain some power or influence.

Another risky approach is to pick a powerful stakeholder whom you will never be able to persuade and confront them quite conspicuously. By setting yourself in opposition, you define your position – and theirs – more clearly. The objective would be to polarise opinions, crystallising support from stakeholders who, up until now, have believed that they could safely hold back from stating their position. If you do win, you get the added benefit of enhancing your power, but beware: this technique is beloved of politicians and it has both made and destroyed careers.

Constructive engagement

An opposite of constructive conflict is constructive engagement (another being destructive conflict!). Constructive engagement is where your engagement process is not simply helpful to you, but also provides added value to the stakeholders with whom you are engaging.

In a project with a large number of near-autonomous stakeholders, each with contractual relationships to a national infrastructure business, successful stakeholder engagement was attributed to three principal factors:

1. The central project team created genuine two-way dialogue between the sponsoring organisation and the stakeholders.
2. All communication was transparent (visible to all) and consistent. Stakeholders could understand why they were being engaged and every discussion or formal communication was consistent.
3. The project team was seen to add value to the process by facilitating communication between the stakeholders, acting as a hub and drawing them together to share common concerns and issues.

Negotiation as soft conflict

The last skill of soft power is negotiation, a ritualised form of conflict where emotion is replaced by process and power is subordinate to skill. Nobody can reasonably think themselves the more or less powerful person at the outset of a negotiation: each party has something the other wants, giving them a unique power base. Power in multi-faceted, so one protagonist may have more hierarchical authority, while another has greater expertise. One may control access to material resources, while another has access to a network of support. You may have a democratic legitimacy, yet I may have a moral authority.

The negotiation process has four simple steps:

1. *Preparation*
   Know what outcome you want and understand as much as you can about your stakeholder. Determine the least acceptable outcome of your negotiation by understanding what your best alternative is. This is known as your 'BATNA' – your best alternative to a negotiated agreement.
   The term 'BATNA' was coined by Roger Fisher and William Ury and is fully described in their magnificent introduction to negotiating, *Getting to Yes*.

2. *Opening*

   When you meet your stakeholder, start by creating a measure of rapport between you, even if it is little more than a formal introduction and a courteous handshake. Negotiation is a social activity and it is important to establish the personal connection first. Open your negotiation by establishing the scope of your stakeholder's authority: can they conclude the negotiation or are you actually negotiating with an intermediary? Then ask the stakeholder to set out their position. Unless your position is very different from what they are expecting, your best advantage is to get them to articulate their objective first.

3. *Bargaining*

   The heart of negotiation is the bargaining stage: trading concessions to reach a position of overlap where both of you can feel that your interests are satisfied. Never offer a concession without seeking one in return and make sure each concession is around half the value of the previous one, or your negotiation will never end.

4. *Close*

   You must close the negotiation. When you sense that agreement is possible, test it out and ask if your stakeholder is ready to agree. If not, you have signalled that you are close to your BATNA, so ask what it would take for them to conclude. Once you have shaken hands and agreed, say no more about the negotiation; stick scrupulously to next steps and pleasantries. Nothing you can say can improve your position, but it can easily create a problem for you.

CASE STUDY

The practitioner was leading a three-month project to determine opportunities for cost savings in a large commercial enterprise. The problem was that this business had three CEOs in 12 months, each with a very different personal style. During this project, the second CEO was in post, but was an interim appointment.

The project manager negotiated commercial terms with the interim CEO, leading to a constant battle to enforce those terms with the succeeding CEO. Never negotiate with an interim if you can possibly avoid it – and if you cannot, be sure to get the agreement in writing.

Hidden Power:
Behavioural Economics

Richard Thaler was a graduate student studying under one of the leading economists of his generation: Sherwin Rosen. Thaler's thesis was 'The Value of Saving a Life: A Market Estimate'. His methodology was coldly analytical: he looked at how much more the labour market would pay people to do high-risk jobs. As you would expect, this involved lots of data-gathering and statistical analysis. But Thaler had a moment of genius: he decided to try asking people about how they valued their lives. This turned out to be a good idea, but the genius was in how he asked the question.

Thaler asked the question in two different ways. As an economist, he knew that logically, the answers to the two questions *ought to be* the same. Yet he still asked some people one question and some the other. And as a rational economist, he was shocked by the answers:

Question 1. When he asked people how much they would be willing to pay to eliminate a 1/1,000 risk of immediate death, the typical answer (in the early 1970s) was less than $200.

Question 2. When he asked people how much they would have to be paid to accept an additional 1/1,000 risk of immediate death, the typical answer (in the early 1970s) was over $50,000.

This was a huge difference, which subsequent experiments have continued to support. The value of a 1/1,000 chance of death is entirely dependent upon how you ask the question.

Thaler went on to coin a number of highly evocative terms, and at the heart of his research is the concept that how we ask questions and set up situations will determine the choices people make. He called this process 'choice architecture'.

Of course, this was not new. Well before the 1970s, shopkeepers knew that how you presented goods determined which ones people would buy. Supermarkets place premium goods at eye level, they put sweets and magazines near the checkout counter and use point of sale advertising, they offer trial packs and free tastings, and they pump the smell of baking bread throughout the store and also into the street.

Why behavioural economics works

The assumption of rationality

Thaler started his economics education in a world where rationality ruled. And the prevailing theories of economics of the time were based on one core assumption: that human beings act rationally when making economic choices. His supervisor, Sherwin Rosen, was a colleague of leading economic theorists of the Chicago School of Economics, which spawned a number of Nobel Prizes in Economics. One of its most powerful theories was 'rational choice theory', which suggests that economic and social actions are carried out by 'rational agents' who are motivated by a rational intention to optimise their positions.

Yet what Thaler had discovered is that so-called rational agents are anything but rational. If they were, then economic incentives would increase altruistic behaviour. After all, if you can do good *and* receive a reward, then this must be more attractive than doing good and not receiving a reward. Health systems rely on donated blood; giving blood is a good thing. So a rational agent would be more likely to give blood if they were paid. In his book *The Gift Relationship*, Richard Titmus shows that this is not so. Comparing the UK, where blood donation is purely voluntary, with the US, where there are financial incentives to donate blood, he found that more people give blood voluntarily than for remuneration. What seems to happen is that the motivation to do good is subverted by the feeling that we are being bribed to do it.

Unlike rational agents, whom Thaler labelled 'econs', human beings are social and moral agents with our decisions anchored in a social and moral context. In this case, a sense of moral obligation has a strong influence over behaviours and choices. This is something moral philosophers have known for a long time, and the study of moral duties is called 'deontology', which holds that some acts are intrinsically right or wrong. We know this and feel a strong pull to act accordingly. For most of us, this is hard-wired into our psychology, and it was to psychology that Thaler gravitated.

The Chicago School may have chalked up many Nobel Prizes in Economics, but sadly, the Nobel Foundation offers no prizes for psychology. So it may have come as a surprise to many when, in 2002, a psychologist won a Nobel Prize. That year's Nobel Prize in Economics recognised the seismic shift in economics which Thaler had spotted and contributed to, and was awarded to Daniel Kahneman 'for having integrated insights from psychological research into economic science, especially concerning human judgment and decision-making under uncertainty'.

System 1 and System 2

Kahneman's fundamental insight was simple: humans are not rational agents. Treating all economic theories as if they are will result in models that are simply wrong. Yet we do behave rationally sometimes, so what is going on?

Kahneman spent many years collaborating closely with his friend and colleague Amos Tversky until the latter's untimely death in 1996. Their research looked at how we make choices and focused on the mental simplifications and shortcuts that we use to find answers, which are called 'heuristics'. These appear to be hard-coded into the way our brains work and are thought to be the cumulative result of our evolutionary history. The problem is that our evolutionary experiences do not always match modern-day conditions. So these simple thought processes often lead to the wrong answers, introducing bias into our thinking.

It is as if our brains have two alternative processes that we can call upon to solve a problem, make a judgement or take a decision. One is entirely rational and thinks through situations afresh, calling upon a dispassionate assessment of all the available information. This is the process we use when we act as rational agents. The other is quick and uses approximations and simplifications, and restricts itself to what it considers to be the salient subset of information. Both ways of thinking serve us well, but in different circumstances. Lots of names have been proposed for these two thinking systems, but I shall follow the choice that Daniel Kahneman makes in his magnificent book that sums up the whole field of research into heuristics and biases that he co-founded with Amos Tversky, *Thinking, Fast and Slow*.

Kahneman adopts the simple terminology proposed by Keith Stanovich and Richard West. He calls the fast thinking, irrational, almost automatic process that draws on experience and intuition 'System 1' and the slower, more deliberate, analytic thinking process 'System 2'. You should not take this description of two systems as suggesting that there are two physically separate parts of the human brain. Our brains work as one complex organ, but the systems represent two modes of its operation, one well-suited to rapid response in familiar surroundings and the other to controlled response to unfamiliar circumstances.

The problem is that System 2 thinking takes a lot of energy, so our lazy, energy-conserving brains would rather give the work to quick, low-energy System 1. This means that we apply System 1 thinking to a large portion of our lives and often to problems for which it is ill-suited. Figure 6.1 below shows how we allocate consideration to these two systems, depending upon our level of motivation to process the information and our ability to process it.

However, research shows that the heuristic System 1 approach is only well-suited to either simple problems or to complex problems where we have

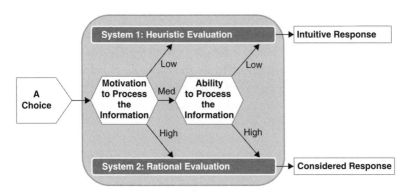

FIGURE 6.1 An heuristic/rational model of thinking

accumulated deep, relevant experience in the way that a tradesperson, artisan or professional does after many years of mastering their craft.

Beyond soft power

At the start of Chapter 5, we introduced the concepts of hard power, economic power and soft power. Thaler's concept of choice architecture and our understanding that System 1 can make rapid decisions based on how a problem is presented to it together suggest a fourth form of power: 'hidden power'.

> **DEFINITION**
>
> *Hidden power*: the ability to influence the choices that System 1 makes.

I choose the term 'hidden power' in recognition of an important popularisation of the subject. In 1957, Vince Packard published an exposé of the American advertising industry, which showed them to be, as I suggested at the start of this chapter, years ahead of the economists. It was called *The Hidden Persuaders* and was about how marketers sought to manipulate our hopes, needs and fears to sell us their clients' goods. In Chapter 2 of this book, Packard makes a statement that pre-empts behavioural economics by at least a decade:

> Finally, the marketers decided it is dangerous to assume that people can be trusted to behave in a rational way.

Packard saw the hidden persuaders as manipulative and, 50 years ahead of concerns over web companies storing and using vast quantities of personal data, made an impassioned case for our right to privacy. The debate about behavioural economics is polarised by the concepts of manipulation and privacy, and we will return to this at the end of the chapter. But, like other tools, behavioural economics can be viewed as morally neutral, its ethics lying in why, when and how we use it.

Why, when and how

System 1 makes mistakes that lead to bias. A common – and arguably *the* most pernicious – example is 'confirmation bias'.

DEFINITION

Confirmation bias: the tendency to focus on information that confirms what we already believe to be true and, consequently, to screen out contradictory evidence.

Confirmation bias is responsible for the persistence of unfounded prejudices and therefore for all of the evils this has unleashed on our societies. Many other heuristic judgements and biases lead us to make decisions that are not good for us. Western governments and, notably, Barack Obama's US administration and the UK's Conservative Party within the 2010 Coalition Government are keen to use behavioural economics and choice architecture to guide people to make choices that are good for them and good for society. Nobody would contend that politicians' choices are morally neutral and definitively correct, but both governments are motivated to do what they believe is right. Where their hidden influence explicitly allows for true freedom of choice, proponents of behavioural economics argue that it is an acceptable means of persuasion. Once again, Thaler coined a memorable term, referring to this kind of influence as a 'nudge'.

DEFINITION

Nudge: a situation or circumstance that predictably shifts behaviours whilst retaining total freedom of choice.

In engaging with stakeholders, you would use the ideas of behavioural economics and choice architecture when you want to push them gently in a direction of your choosing, but you will do so in a way that is wholly free of coercion and entirely respectful of their right to choose.

In a slew of popular books led, naturally, by Thaler's own book, with co-author Cass Sunstein, *Nudge: Improving Decisions about Health, Wealth and Happiness* and also Dan Ariely's *Predictably Irrational: The Hidden Forces that Shape Our Decisions* you can read about the techniques of choice architecture and the many ways that System 1 leads us to behave irrationally. In the next section, we will look at some examples of these, but first, let's look at the process for designing your choice architecture.

The process of applying behavioural economics to stakeholder engagement

We have a perfectly good process for stakeholder engagement illustrated on page 20 (Figure 1.4). So let us apply the same process to the specific task of designing a choice architecture.

Step 1: identify

The first step is to identify which stakeholders' behaviours you want to influence, their existing behaviours and attitudes, and the goals you want to work towards.

Step 2: analyse

Now consider how your stakeholders think and act. What motivates them, what choices do they have and what constraints are they under?

Step 3: plan

Now review what you know about behavioural economics and determine what approach – or combination of approaches – is likely to shift behaviours in the way that you want, whilst retaining genuine freedom of choice for your stakeholders.

Step 4: act

Once you have designed your behavioural interventions, put them into place. Ensure that you do so with integrity, such that they are fully consistent with overt messages and that you and your team are visibly making the choices that are consistent with your messages and nudges.

Step 5: review

Is it working? This is not just a pragmatic question of whether your nudges are shifting behaviours in the way you planned, but also whether stakeholders are feeling positively engaged and content with their choices or whether they are feeling manipulated.

If your nudges are not working, revert to step 2 and analyse why not, before re-designing (or possibly abandoning) your choice architecture.

Practical techniques

There are so many techniques documented that no single book – let alone a single chapter – could do justice to them. And even within a chapter, where I am being selective, I need to organise my examples and impose some structure upon them to prevent it becoming a giant list. Figure 6.2 below sets out the ten categories I shall use and arranges them in terms of the psychological closeness to your stakeholder. We shall start with the furthest away and work our way in from the stakeholder's external environment to their innermost preferences.

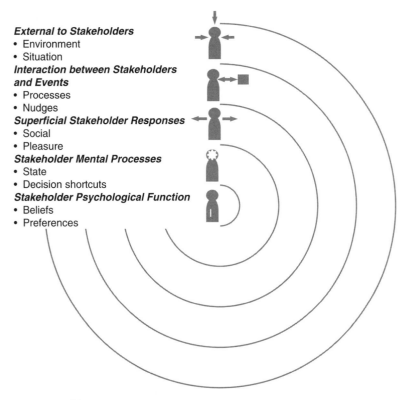

External to Stakeholders
• Environment
• Situation
Interaction between Stakeholders and Events
• Processes
• Nudges
Superficial Stakeholder Responses
• Social
• Pleasure
Stakeholder Mental Processes
• State
• Decision shortcuts
Stakeholder Psychological Function
• Beliefs
• Preferences

FIGURE 6.2 / Levels of hidden influence

External to stakeholders

Environment

1. *Physical environment*
   If I perceive you as having more authority than me, it lends weight to your ideas, increasing your influence. Use your physical environment to convey authority, first by inviting me into your space and then choosing your space to further emphasise your authority. Books and

files indicate access to knowledge, hospitality indicates confidence, and the trappings of power (large desk, individual office, secretary outside) speak for themselves. Sportspeople all know the advantage that home ground brings.

2. *Psychological environment*

Can you enhance the impact of the physical environment where you meet? Researchers at Newcastle University found that people were more likely to contribute payment for the use of milk in teas and coffees to an honesty box when the payment notice included a picture of eyes than when it included a picture of flowers. In June 2013, Thames Valley Police in England followed other forces in introducing two life-size cardboard cut-out images of police officers to act as a deterrent to shoplifting. Bangalore City Police in India use similar cut-outs to deter traffic violations.

3. *Social environment*

We feel so compelled to fit in with our circle of friends and the other people immediately around us that pressure to conform overrides economic or moral pressures. In an experiment conducted for her Master's thesis, Dr Jessica Nolan and her colleagues hung energy conservation messages onto the doors of 1,207 households in San Marcos, California. These were split into five different messages: a control message with factual information only, three messages appealing to environmental concerns, social responsibility and saving money, and the final message comparing the householder with their neighbours. Only the last of these resulted in a reduction in daily energy consumption.

Conclusion: the environment that you place around your stakeholders can substantially influence their choices. Think about where you will meet them, the psychological cues that you can introduce and how you can use the perceptions and choices of other stakeholders.

Situation

1. *Priming*

The words, sights and sounds we are exposed to can influence subsequent choices and behaviours – a fact well known to magicians and mind-readers, as well as to advertisers. Simply asking people if they intend to change their car over the next six months increased purchase rates by 37 per cent. So, alerting stakeholders to relevant information such as the place, date and time of a meeting, and asking them if they will attend can increase turnout. However, one enquiry will be enough. Research conducted by Vicki Morwitz of New York University and Eric Johnson and David Schmittlein of the University of Pennsylvania found that asking more than once did not increase purchase rates in people who had expressed a positive intention to change their car, but they did decrease purchase rates for those who said they did not intend to change their car (see V. Morwitz, E. Johnson and D. Schmittlein (1993) Does Measuring Intent Change Behaviour?', *Journal of Consumer Research*, 20(1): 46–61).

2. *Availability*

Recent events weigh heavily on our decision-making, introducing biases that result, for example, in many people driving to work shortly after a train accident. This matters because roads are far less safe than railways, and the increase in accidents usually leads to a higher casualty toll on the roads in the weeks after the rail accident than had been caused by the accident itself. Likewise, the immediate discomfort of an unpleasant task, like cleaning the kitchen or mowing the lawn, often results in procrastination. This sensation is far more readily available to our consciousness than the pleasure of a clean kitchen or a neat garden.

3. *Salience*

When something happens a lot, like car accidents, we stop noticing them: the press does not report them and they become unremarkable. We notice what is novel or relevant to us and it figures more highly in our decision-making. Plane crashes and lottery winners are examples of novel events that lead us to over-estimate their likelihood of occurring. In April 2005, the *Financial Times* reported that the Royal Mail had reduced absenteeism by entering all staff with no sick leave for six months into a lottery, with the chance to win a car or holiday vouchers. Sickness absence dropped to 5.7 per cent from 6.4 per cent in the same period in the previous year.

Conclusion: the information that stakeholders have available will affect their choices. By placing information into their awareness, emphasising recent events and creating emotionally charged examples, you can direct where your stakeholders' attention will go.

Interaction between stakeholders and events

Process

1. *Messenger*

   One of the most powerful ways in which a message can influence is through the messenger; if you trust, believe or like the messenger, the message will be more likely to persuade you. So cultivate your own trustworthiness, credibility and likeability. Or, better yet, find ways to have your message delivered by someone else, an opinion leader perhaps, who has these characteristics in the eyes of your stakeholder.

2. *Involvement*

   One of the most important reasons why stakeholders choose to do or not do something is whether they believe that they can have any influence over its success: we need to feel in control. Involving stakeholders in your decisions and your actions is one of the most important ways through which you can get their compliance.

3. *Commitments*

   When we make a plan to do something, it takes on a sense of reality. When we go further and share that plan with someone else, we are making a commitment. If your stakeholder is a person of integrity, then, when they make a commitment, they will feel a strong psychological pressure to honour it. This is the basis of 'foot in the door' tactics like this example: some homeowners (the big request group) were asked to display either a large 'Drive Carefully' sign on their front lawn, while others (the small request group) were offered a three-inch safe driving sticker for their window. While nearly all residents agreed to the sticker, only 17 per cent agreed to the large sign. Yet, when the small request group were subsequently asked to host the large sign, 76 per cent agreed. Getting a small agreement – especially if you can make it conspicuous – will help you later on in getting a bigger agreement from your stakeholders. If, however, you ask too much at the outset, you will be unlikely to achieve consent.

Conclusion: when you want to influence stakeholders' decisions, think about the process you apply: who should do the persuading, how to engage the stakeholders and give them a sense of control over events, and what visible commitments you can get from them as a step on the way to gaining their agreement to a bigger request.

Context

1. *Norms*

   Societies have norms of behaviour and, much as we like to think of ourselves as individuals, few of us feel comfortable stepping outside of these norms. So remind your stakeholders which norms apply and anticipate that many of them will fall into line with these. One of the most successful campaigns to raise tax revenues is a letter to people who owe money telling them, factually, that most people in their area pay their tax on time. As a result, payment rates rose from 68 to 83 per cent. In the UK, there was great resistance in the 1970s when it became compulsory to wear seatbelts in cars. Now this it is the norm and almost nobody questions this aspect of the law.

2. *Defaults*

   Since people are intrinsically lazy, we often assume that other people have made the right choices, and accept default options without questioning them. In countries where the default on organ donation is that everyone is a donor unless they opt out, they have more donors than where opting in is the requirement. The same effect appears with opt-in or opt-out pension schemes and when governments choose defaults that they know will benefit people and society, Thaler and Sunstein describe this in their book *Nudge* as 'liberal paternalism'.

3. *Incentives*

   I know that this sounds like economic power, but bear with me... Incentives can work, even when their absolute value is far less than your stakeholder would normally change their behaviour for. Would you expect a highly paid hospital doctor to change their behaviour in return for a \$10 (around £6) voucher for coffee? Writing in the *New York Times Magazine* (24 September 2006), Stephen J. Dubner and Steven D. Levitt discussed the case of Los Angeles urologist Leon Bender, who wanted to improve hand-washing practices at his hospital, but found that nothing he tried, from emails to faxes to posters, would persuade doctors. So his team gave out bottles of disinfectant hand wash as doctors arrived in the car park and then tried to catch people using the hand wash. When they did, they awarded the \$10 Starbucks card as a reward. Compliance rose from 65 to 80 per cent. Small incentives seem to act as a reminder to do the right thing.

In the example given above, in case you are wondering what they did about the last 20 per cent, they took cultures from the hands of members of the Chief of Staff Advisory Committee – mostly the hospital's top doctors – and displayed images of the resulting bacterial colonies. Disgust is a powerful emotion and it too acted as an incentive, raising compliance to nearly 100 per cent.

Conclusion: one way to prompt choices from your stakeholders is to show them that the choice is an easy one – conforming to standard behaviours (norms) or to standard choices (defaults). And you can amplify this by offering token incentives that act as a reminder of the right choices.

Stakeholder responses

Social

We have already seen how you can use your social environment and the norms of your society to sway choices, but there are other aspects of our social natures that you can also bring to bear:

1. *Obligation*

   We are motivated by a need to do the right thing and to be seen to do the right thing. One valuable component that you can employ is our need to reciprocate a generous gesture. This is not about the corrupt procurement of favours, but by doing small favours and granting concessions, you pre-dispose your stakeholders to look kindly on your requests for favours and concessions. One easy favour to grant a stakeholder is to bring them 'inside the tent'. By sharing a confidence about a change in advance, you make them a part of the changes, creating a sense of complicity and loyalty.

2. *Affiliation*

   Bringing a stakeholder inside the tent also creates a perception of shared interests – which makes them part of your group. This goes even deeper. We know that when people are regarded as part of another group, we are more likely to discount their feelings and even act towards them with barbarity. The psychologist Albert Bandura has shown that the way experimental subjects overhear the researchers talking about a group of people will affect how severely they are prepared to treat them. When the researchers refer to a group of students as nice, the subjects will dole out far lesser punishments for errors than when they are described as animals.

3. *Reputation*

In a group or society, our reputation matters to us very much and we will choose actions that avoid any loss of face. Your reputation is an important component of your soft power – exploiting my concern for my own reputation is an aspect of your hidden power. If I make a commitment publicly, for example, I will act to maintain it and, better yet, if you can get me to make a written commitment, I am almost certain to stick to it.

Conclusion: stakeholders are social beings and you can use their desire to fulfil obligations and maintain their reputations to nudge behaviours in your favour. Making them a part of your project brings them into your circle, inclining them towards supporting your project, rather than opposing it, and making criticisms privately rather than publicly.

Pleasure

1. *Fun*

People will do things that are fun, so how can you make your stakeholder engagement fun for your stakeholders? Prototypes, pilot simulations and even games can teach project and change management teams a lot about the processes and technology they are implementing, and can engage stakeholders in a fun activity. Fun can also change behaviours: Volkswagen has a whole team and a global competition designed to identify and test ways to make safety and environmentally sound behaviours fun. The website at www.thefuntheory.com has a number of great examples like bottle banks that play sounds and give scores, in-car entertainment that only works when seatbelts are on, and stairs that play musical notes to lure people off the nearby escalator to get some exercise.

2. *Competition*

And after fun comes competition – we love games also because we love to win, so how can you harness stakeholders' competitive natures to support your initiative? Examples include canvassing ideas and submitting them to peer voting, and making waste-paper bins like basketball hoops.

3. *Mastery*

And after winning comes mastery. Acquiring deep expertise is a primary motivator for many people in the workplace, so look for ways to engage your stakeholders in ways that make them feel they are learning, acquiring new skills and deepening existing ones.

Conclusion: play, winning and excelling are deep drives in us. If you can harness these drives, you can have a profound impact on your stakeholders' choices and behaviours.

Stakeholder mental processes

Mental state

1. *Mood*

   Psychologists have a specific term, 'affect', to describe the mood or emotion associated with a specific experience, stimulus or idea. Emotional responses have a big impact on choices, often shutting down our rational System 2 thinking processes, resulting in irrational decisions. This is particularly the case when we are tired or stressed. At these times, we have reduced motivation and the mental capacity to process ideas rationally (see Figure 6.1 above). Consequently, high-integrity influencing must take place when your stakeholders are in a good emotional, mental and physical state, or you risk an automatic response that is ill-thought out and that they may later regret. Quite simply, step away from an argument with an angry stakeholder, don't try to persuade a frightened stakeholder, avoid cajoling a miserable stakeholder and never expect to properly influence a stakeholder who is tired or run-down.

2. *Expectation*

   Our past experiences lead us to anticipate the future, with the commonest bias being to expect more of the same. If a past act, like participating in a consultation or leading a team, has made your stakeholder feel good, then gently reminding them of that ('I am looking forward to more of your comments at next week's forum' or 'I hope your new team will be as successful as last time') will boost their commitment. However, we don't always expect more of the same…

3. *Optimism*

   Your level of optimism or pessimism has a profound effect on your judgements and choices. Choices often create a self-fulfilling cycle. High levels of enthusiasm and optimism tend to generate 'optimistic bias', where we anticipate best possible outcomes without properly evaluating risk. 'Pessimism bias' arises from demotivation and depressed moods, and results in over-cautious choices. When you engage with stakeholders, you need to manage their levels of optimism to ensure that they approach the world with the right balance of caution and confidence.

Optimism or pessimism biases can lead to wholly unrealistic expectations, called 'the gambler's run bias'. Here, despite compelling evidence, we expect our luck – or the world – to change. Pessimistically, despite continued success, we anticipate imminent failure; optimistically, despite evidence to the contrary, we constantly expect things to succeed. The principal danger of these is that the sense of fate means people often do nothing to take control of their circumstances – like an addicted gambler.

Conclusion: if you fail to take account of your stakeholders' mental states, you risk engaging the worst aspects of irrational System 1 thinking. Engage stakeholders when they are at their best and help them to balance caution and confidence by avoiding the traps of over-optimism and excessive risk aversion yourself.

Mental shortcuts

1. *Heuristics*

   Mental shortcuts, known as heuristics, occur when System 1 takes control. Yet some shortcuts get us to the wrong place: here's a typical example. A bat and ball cost £1.10 in total. The bat costs £1 more than the ball. How much does the ball cost? Shane Frederick found that most people let System 1 do the work and get an instant answer: 10 pence. But this answer is wrong; check it. The correct answer is…

   Because our brains evolved in very different conditions from the world we live in today, sometimes the shortcuts it takes get us to the wrong place, so you need to be sure that your stakeholders are able to engage System 2 by warning them of 'obvious' answers that are wrong. This stimulates curiosity and so motivates them to engage System 2 to do the work and check out the correct answer for themselves… as I hope you did.

2. *Framing*

   How information or a question is presented has a massive effect on how we respond to it. Tools like PowerPoint and Keynote are particularly dangerous because they allow us to present information in a highly polished way. Yet the more immaculate the presentation, the less likely your audience is to question it. This has led the US Army to deprecate slide presentations of information used in decision-making. Spreadsheets and project plans also garner less careful scrutiny when beautifully formatted, so ensure that draft documents look like unfinished work.

3. *Comparisons*

Shops use framing powerfully to influence buying decisions. Here are two examples from recent shopping trips. £30 for a scarf or a tie is, you might think, expensive. But if you have just decided to buy a £300 suit and the salesperson shows you two or three of them to look at, which would all set off your new suit nicely, the £30 seems a lot less significant. People will haggle over £50 on the price of a new sofa, but will not haggle over the last £500 on the price of a home – yet £500 is £500. Once your stakeholder has made a big commitment, it is a good time to ask for another, related, small commitment: 'While we are on the subject…'

Another shopkeeper's trick you can apply is the 'middle option gambit'. You want a new camera for family holidays, so the retailer shows you a £500 all-singing, all-dancing model. 'That's far too much money', you say, 'and I don't need such a sophisticated model.' 'Well,' says the shopkeeper, 'I have these two models, the basic at £50 and the Sport XK at £150.' Few people will go for the most basic and risk appearing to be a cheapskate, so the middle option is usually favoured. Ask your stakeholder to accept an extravagant, excessive position that you know they are unlikely to adopt before offering a choice that falls short of reasonable and another, middle way.

By the way, have you noticed that model names of cameras, cars and all sorts of consumer goods are designed to indicate which ones are exciting and therefore 'suitable' for most customers? Letters like X and Z carry excitement, so think carefully about how you label concepts, ideas and initiatives. There is a reason why nobody sells condoms in 'small'.

Conclusion: System 1 is easily influenced. When you present information to help a stakeholder make a decision, think about whether it is System 1 or System 2 that you want them to engage and design the process accordingly.

Stakeholder psychological function

Beliefs

1. *Over-confidence*

Similar to optimism bias, which we saw above, is over-confidence bias. This is over-confidence in our abilities and in our plans. A total of

93 per cent of respondents in a US survey put themselves in the top
50 per cent of drivers for skill and 88 per cent for safety, for example.
Most professional investors believe they can beat the market in picking
stocks when actually most are outperformed by random selection.
When it comes to project plans, over-confidence often combines with
'planning fallacy' – a tendency to under-estimate how long things will
take. Over-confidence then leads them to believe their plans. The two
combine to create what is sometimes known as 'Hofstadter's Law',
which appears in the Douglas Hofstadter's astonishing book *Gödel,
Escher, Bach: An Eternal Golden Braid*.

DEFINITION

Hofstadter's Law: it always takes longer than you expect, even
when you take into account Hofstadter's Law.

2. *Mental accounting*

   Hotel breakfasts are expensive – at one I stayed in, it was £12.00 for
   a bowl of cereal, a slice of toast or a stale croissant and a cup of tea
   or coffee. At the café a few doors away, better coffee, cereal, a bacon
   sandwich and a muffin came to £11.20. When you book a hotel,
   though, you pay for a room and, if offered breakfast, that goes into a
   'mental account' with the room; now £112 for a room and breakfast
   seems fine. If you have only booked the room and you go down to
   breakfast to find it will cost you £12, that seems expensive and you will
   consider walking a few yards to the café.

   We keep account of different things in different mental buckets. If you
   can guide your stakeholder to use the right bucket, the reaction you
   get will be very different from that which will result from the wrong
   bucket.

3. *Self-image*

   We don't like to make mistakes and still less do we like to admit to
   them. This means that, even when we have made a mistake, many of
   us go on defending our actions. This is not just capricious, however.
   Often our rationalisation of a wrong choice is not to fool others, but
   to persuade ourselves. If you want me to change my mind, you need
   to help me save face. Offer me a reason why my judgement was right
   when I made it, but needs to change now, in the light of something

I did not know about. Now, I am not changing my mind at all – I am making a new decision based on new evidence.

Conclusion: you will be far more effective in persuading stakeholders when you take account of how their brains will process decisions – how they place them in one bucket or another, how confident they feel about their choices and how their decisions will affect the way they think about themselves.

Preferences

1. *Habit*

   'That's the way we have always done things.' 'If it ain't broke, don't fix it.' The power of habit has become crystallised in some of the most prevalent organisational clichés. Habits are hard to change because it takes mental effort to take on new behaviours, and in doing so, we feel we are exposing ourselves to risk. So fear of failure figures strongly in our desire to stick with what we know. This is a key factor for any change agent to be aware of. If you need to over-ride habits, the path of least resistance is not to challenge them, but to provide gentle incentives to adopt new behaviours, which will then themselves become new habits supplementing and, later, supplanting the old ones.

2. *Present*

   Immediate gratification is a strong bias of System 1, whilst it is System 2 that exerts self-control: one marshmallow now or two in ten minutes? People are often unable or unwilling to do the proper mental calculations to evaluate alternative investments, so look at an immediate saving as preferable, even if the long-term interest payments render the price exorbitant. In persuading stakeholders of long-term benefits over short-term losses, you need to find representations of the facts that will appeal to System 1: physical analogues and demonstrations. This is why TV shows that help people with over-eating don't just tell people about the implications of their habits over a year, they show them, by piling up a year's supply of chips, burgers and fizzy drinks. It is why they don't just talk about the percentage of fat in those chips and burgers, they bring in a wheelbarrow full of melted lard.

3. *Loss aversion*

   Why do people feel an urge to replace a book they have lost, even if they have already read it? Once something is ours, its loss feels uncomfortable. This is one principal reason why people resist change: they would need to give up the past. In fact, experiment after experiment shows that once we feel we own something, we place a far higher value on it than when we are considering buying it.

The classic experiment was conducted by Daniel Kahneman, Richard Thaler and Jack Knetsch ((1991) 'Anomalies: The Endowment Effect, Loss Aversion, and Status Quo Bias', *Journal of Economic Perspectives*, 5(1): 193–206). They gave half of a group of students mugs branded with the university insignia. They then asked them to set a price at which they would be willing to sell their mugs. The other half of the group were asked to examine a mug and then give a price at which they were willing to buy one. The difference was marked, with sellers setting a price ($5.25) around twice that of buyers. When you are dealing with stakeholders, it pays to be very aware of what they will perceive that you are asking them to give up and to be mindful that they will probably set a very different, higher value on it from you.

Conclusion: perhaps the most powerful stakeholder urges are their aversion to loss, their comfort with habit and their preference for immediate over future rewards. If you fail to account for these, you will fail. Yet, if you build them into your engagement strategies, you will enhance your chances of success.

The ethics of stakeholder engagement

Towards the start of this chapter, we defined a nudge as a situation or circumstance that predictably shifts behaviours whilst retaining total freedom of choice. One way of looking at a nudge is as a way to encourage your stakeholders to access their true preferences despite any mental biases. As soon as you encroach upon their freedom of choice, however, you are starting to manipulate your stakeholders. This kind of subtle coercion is more of a shove than a nudge.

Getting the ethics right is not easy. Even a simple choice of default option can raise ethical concerns. What *should* the default be on organ donation? Patients may benefit if there are more donors, because we choose an opt-out régime, and maybe that means society does too – but is it the *right* thing to do?

Behavioural economics certainly offers us tools to help our stakeholders make the right decisions. But it fails to guide us as to what the right decisions are. Consequently, how it is being used in public life is attracting much debate, which you need to consider when you choose to (or choose not to) apply its ideas.

Max Clarkson was an important early thinker about business ethics and stakeholder theory. He developed seven principles of stakeholder management, often referred to as the 'Clarkson Principles'. These were drafted with corporate social responsibility in mind and apply across all business processes (see *Principles of Stakeholder Management*. Toronto: Clarkson Centre for Business Ethics, 1999). In Appendix 5 I have provided my own set of six commitments for ethical stakeholder engagement in the form of a charter. I invite you to sign it, to share it (you can download a copy from www.theinfluenceagenda.co.uk) and to encourage colleagues to sign it too.

A Dozen Reasons Why You're Wrong: Handling Resistance

The practitioner was leading a project to re-design business processes across a portion of a business, following successful strategy development. His stakeholder group was made up of a dysfunctional management team who did not like one another and who failed to work well together.

The implementation team needed to challenge entrenched thinking about business processes, but every time they tried to do so, one member or another of the management team would get angry. Individually, stakeholders were amenable; in the group, reactions were irate and unpredictable.

The project team had failed to recognise the level of discontent in the team. The adverse reactions had deeper roots than the current intervention.

It is a common situation that reactions to change are linked to history rather than the change itself, and that individual stakeholder reactions are not the whole story; it is also about how they interact. People are not independent of their context and of one another, and are different in groups from how they are on a one-to-one basis.

Perhaps the most feared aspect of stakeholder engagement is dealing with resistance. We sense the potential for the situation to escalate into conflict and few people would welcome that. Yet we also know that resistance is all-but-inevitable. This knowledge can therefore prevent us from properly engaging with stakeholders for fear of the resistance that we will, at some point, encounter.

Resistance to change is most often a result of System 1 processing. This is not to say that it cannot arise from a rational analysis of the situation, but this at least can be countered readily with evidence and reasoning. And often, System 2 is right: resistance is sometimes rational and appropriate, in which case, if you respect your stakeholder, you must also respect their position. We will return to this later on.

When, however, System 1 is in control, it is often operating from a simple 'status quo bias' – an unreasoned preference to keep things as they are. It can be explained as the cumulative effect of a number of other, more fundamental biases, some of which we encountered in Chapter 6. The first is 'existence bias', whereby we assume that, because something already exists, it must be legitimate. This is enhanced by the 'longevity effect': the longer something has existed, the better it must be. We also prefer what we are familiar with, so we are comfortable with the status quo too. This familiarity principle is most often called the 'mere exposure effect'.

A final component of status quo bias is something we encountered in Chapter 6 (page 154): loss aversion. We value what we might gain in a different way from the way we value what we might lose, creating a marked asymmetry. In a change that is neutral between benefit and burden, we value the burden more highly than the benefit, leaving a subjective assessment that the loss exceeds the gain. A change must therefore be significantly beneficial for the diminished perception of benefit to outweigh the enhanced sense of loss. This is particularly the case when the change is irreversible, creating a heightened fear of regret.

Not all aspects of the status quo bias are irrational, however. It is further strengthened where stakeholders do not believe they have all of the information they need. The perception that the status quo is better understood leaves them believing that 'no change' is the safe option. And if they do have the information, stakeholders often find the mental discipline of evaluating it too daunting or, indeed, too difficult; again making the status quo an easy default. See, for example, Figure 6.1 in Chapter 6.

Not all people are equally resistant to change. Shaul Oreg at Cornell University has identified four factors that reliably predict the level of resistance a person will show to change (see (2003) 'Resistance to Change: Developing an Individual Differences Measure', *Journal of Applied Psychology*, 88(4): 680–93). These will later give us a way into how do deal with some specific forms of resistance. The four things that pre-dispose a stakeholder to resist change are as follows:

1. A preference for routine and things that are familiar.
2. A tendency to feel uncomfortable and become stressed when plans change.
3. A preference for sticking to a plan once it is made.
4. A discomfort with changing their mind.

These factors – our natural pre-disposition to prefer the status quo and the fact that some stakeholders will resist more – mean that we can anticipate a measure of resistance with certainty; it is natural. So there is no point in deprecating those who resist or in shying away from engaging with them constructively.

WISE WORDS FROM REAL PRACTITIONERS

You get what you expect: if you expect to be attacked, you interpret challenge as an attack.

This leads me to Stakeholder Rule Number 5 and the Golden Rule of Resistance: *always respect your resisters*.

This chapter is about how to handle their resistance in a respectful and positive manner that will deliver real progress.

The onion model of resistance

Before you can handle resistance, you need to be able to recognise what is happening and understand the nature of the resistance you are receiving.

This will give you the basis for dealing with it appropriately – which may, of course, be to accept it and not actively deal with it. Your first priority is therefore to get it out in the open. Being respectful means you will need to see through your stakeholder's surface behaviours, which may be unhelpful and even seem disrespectful to you, your colleagues or your organisation. Take the time to listen hard and find out what is really going on in their head and their heart. Allow yourself to hear what is going on underneath the emotion and don't let your stakeholder's difficulties in expressing themselves clearly get in the way of your interpretation. Finally, it is worth saying that your stakeholder may know something that you don't, so open yourself to their insights. In doing this, you will become curious, leading to greater objectivity and a more respectful style of dialogue.

Figure 7.1 below sets out my basic model of how stakeholders resist change. It is called the 'onion model of resistance' because each time

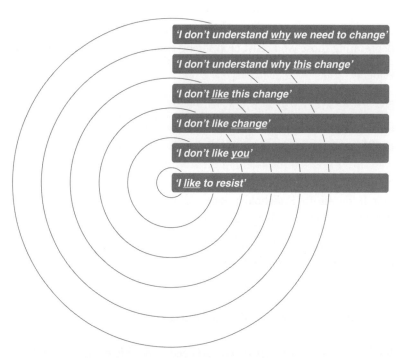

FIGURE 7.1   The onion model of resistance to change

you peel off and deal with one layer of resistance, there seems to be another one beneath it. And each successive layer gets hotter and more uncomfortable to deal with.

In the sections that follow, we will look at each level of resistance, first as a diagnostic for the source and nature of the resistance, and then to see what practical approach you can take to handling that resistance.

'I don't <u>understand</u> why we need to change'

'If it ain't broke, don't fix it' is a perfectly reasonable strategy. And if you don't know that the system, process or culture is broken, then resistance is perfectly reasonable. The problem is that external factors change constantly and the suitability of the way organisations work diminishes slowly over time, as competitors gain a commercial advantage, technology advances and regulations change. At some point, somebody in your organisation has realised that change is necessary and initiates action. The fact that your stakeholders are unaware of this pressure for change explains the first reason why they will resist.

So if this is the nature of the resistance you encounter, you need to demonstrate that not changing is not an option. You need to frame the evidence in a way that it will make real sense to them – at a gut level as well as an intellectual level. If you can do so, find a way to get them involved in evaluating the status quo and making the case that change is necessary. However, don't under-estimate the power of an attachment to the present and prepare yourself for the argument that there is time: we can wait. Often rumours get out and nothing happens, so there will be a natural scepticism that change will happen soon and this will give your stakeholder's System 1 an excuse to not engage with the change. So demonstrate to them that there is a clear and present threat and that the pressure to do something is imminent.

Another problem you may encounter is the 'oh, but I'm different' response. Everyone thinks that they are a special case, that their department is different, that their organisation is in some way special. This is another way that System 1 protects us from having to face reality and engage System 2. You have to show your stakeholders that the need for change is not just real, not just imminent, but will very much impact them.

'I don't understand why <u>this</u> change'

The second level of resistance starts from an acceptance that change is necessary, but questions why you (or your colleagues or superiors) have chosen the approach that you have. The best corrective to this is to engage your stakeholders in designing the response to the pressures you are under, but you can rarely involve all of your stakeholders. Take time to explain the reasoning and use demonstrations, prototypes and graphics to support your argument. Here is where other stakeholders who have been involved in the process can really help you.

Lack of understanding can take two forms: simple and subtle. Simple lack of understanding is no more than your failure to communicate in a way that your stakeholder understands. If at first you don't succeed... try a *different* approach. Too many poor communicators just repeat the failed message again and again, blaming their stakeholder for not 'getting it'. This is not what we described as the process for effective communication at the start of Chapter 4. Instead, you need to take responsibility for your communication, listen to how your stakeholder expresses their confusion and try again in a different way.

A subtle lack of understanding occurs when your stakeholder understands what you are saying, but does not understand it in the way that you intended. Consequently, they get the wrong impression and cannot understand why you would make the choice you have made. This misunderstanding happens a lot, so you need to be alert for it by checking from time to time what your stakeholders understand to be the case and addressing miscommunication as soon as you detect it.

'I don't <u>like</u> this change'

In many ways, this is the most important level, although it is not the toughest. Let us look at the three scenarios that can give rise to this form of resistance.

Scenario 1: status quo bias

Change is uncomfortable and the one you will be dealing with now will be no different. Your stakeholder may be better off, but does not yet know it or believe it. System 1 has jumped in before they make the time for a rational assessment. Loss aversion has focused your stakeholder on the cost of their losses – or their fears of losses – which are crowding out the benefits from their attention. There are all sorts of reasons why your stakeholder has succumbed to status quo bias, like loss of security, economic loss, impact on relationships or simple uncertainty. If you want to handle this constructively, you have to patiently chip away at these, opening the space for System 2 to engage. This is where appropriate and ethical nudges can play a part (see Chapter 6).

Scenario 2: your stakeholder will be genuinely worse off

Of course, sometimes, your stakeholder believes they will be worse off because they will lose out financially, need to re-train, have to move location or possibly lose their job. They have analysed the evidence correctly and this is an entirely rational stance to take. The reality of big organisations is that there are a lot of stakeholders – take a look at Appendix 2 for an indication of just how many. And in designing change, you and your colleagues will have tried to optimise the situation and balance the needs of all of your stakeholders. But this does not mean that everyone will be better off; sometimes there will be losers. If this weren't true, the changes would probably have happened sooner. If this stakeholder is one of the losers, there is only one thing you can do with integrity: look them in the eye and say 'you're right'. Remember Stakeholder Rule Number 3: *honesty is not the best policy… it is the only policy.*

Do what you can to help them. Deploy whatever resources are available and guide them to the advice they need – even support them – but never tell them they will be better off if you know (or even suspect) that they will not.

Scenario 3: your stakeholder believes the organisation will be worse off

Sometimes this form of resistance has nothing to do with whether your stakeholder will be better off, worse off or unaffected by the change. They have spotted a problem with what you are doing or how you are doing it and they are genuinely concerned that it will be damaging to the organisation or its other stakeholders. They are trying to give you a warning and it is your responsibility to listen. It is not your responsibility to take their advice, which may be right or wrong, but it is your responsibility to learn as much as you can, evaluate it with care and submit it to due consideration by the right people. Sometimes all that resistance means is that your stakeholder has concerns and they want to be listened to and taken seriously. Providing that respectful ear is a big part of good stakeholder engagement.

'I don't like <u>change</u>'

At the start of this chapter, we introduced Shaul Oreg's research into the four factors that dispose some people to be more resistant to change. Each of them provides a reason why some people don't like change. Indeed, Oreg's research shows that these factors, while different, are often correlated with one another. This means that often, come one, come all. Your stakeholders may not like change due to the following reasons.

'I don't like a break in <u>routine</u>'

If this is the case, place your emphasis on the new routines that will emerge. Acknowledge the temporary break in routine, but place it in the context of a shift towards a new form of stability. Show how old routines are already being disrupted and how this will only continue and grow unless a new way of working is developed and implemented smoothly. Seek their advice on how to make the transition as smooth and effective as possible.

'I get <u>stressed</u> at the thought of change'

The feelings and physiological reactions of stress arise from a sense of not being in control. Your priority here is to make your stakeholder feel that they are in control by genuinely involving them and giving them a part in the decisions that need to be made. This does not mean a big part and in all of the decisions – all they need is enough participation to feel they have some control over their future. Give them options that you can honour, but not so many that they will feel anxiety over the choice. Spell out what the options mean so that the evaluation process is as straightforward for them as you can make it.

'I feel uncomfortable with <u>sudden</u> changes'

Stakeholders who hate to have plans disrupted need plans and a long lead time, so show them that the changes are thoroughly planned out and that you are informing them a long way in advance. As plans will inevitably be modified as your project proceeds, make the process of altering the plan a part of the plan by scheduling review points, announcing updates at the first opportunity and, where possible, casting them as refinements to the plan in the light of improved knowledge rather than as changes to the plan.

'Once I have <u>made up my mind</u>, I like to stick to it'

Oreg refers to this as 'cognitive rigidity' and notes that some people don't change their mind easily. Of his four factors, this has the lowest correlation to resistance to change, reflecting, I suspect, that cognitive rigidity must involve our rational and reasoning System 2. If you want System 2 to reconsider the evidence, you need to overcome System 1's quick intervention, which protects System 2 from having to do new work. Do this by providing a good reason why System 2 needs to re-engage. The easiest way is to present new evidence rather than rely on new arguments about old facts, as that way your stakeholder's need to save face is addressed too: they don't need to change their mind, they only need to make a new choice resulting from the new information.

Not everyone is equally pre-disposed to resist, but we all do sometimes. Fundamentally, 'I don't like change' is about fear – fear that we won't be able to cope fully with the change… fear of failure. The second and third of Oreg's four factors, the emotional reaction and short-term focus, are fundamentally about emotional states and fear is arguably the most powerful emotion. Fear arises from beliefs about the implications of change, which often arise from snap judgements made by System 1. They are therefore often faulty beliefs that you need to address if you are to overcome the stakeholder's resistance.

One belief is 'I don't know how to change'. This may be true or false, but either way, the way to deal with this is with training, support and guidance. Listen carefully to discover what aspects concerns your stakeholder: it may sometimes be the simple mechanical processes that they will need to learn, but it can equally be the social, organisational, cultural or emotional demands that the change will place on them.

Another common belief, which is usually faulty, that gets in the way is 'I don't believe I can change'. Yet we have all changed massively. It is a generalisation that this most often arises among longer-serving staff and team members, but it is often true. Addressing this requires more personal support – from you or from a 'transition buddy'. Look to undermine the belief with counter-examples from their own experience or from those of colleagues with whom they will identify.

'I don't like you'

The greatest obstacle to change is often the way our past experiences of change affect our attitudes and how we cope. 'I don't like you' is rarely personal; about *you*. It is a reflection of how your stakeholder feels about the way change was handled at some earlier point in their career, which they are projecting onto you and how you are dealing with it. You need to show your stakeholder that, whatever the failings were the last time around, you will ensure things will be different this time... and you need to demonstrate why they should believe you through your absolutely consistent ethical behaviour.

'I don't like you' is about history – most often history of experiences with change. But it could also be about the stakeholder's experiences with the organisation, the managers or anything else. Maybe it is about how they felt when they got up that morning. Whichever it is, 'I don't like you' is not about the change itself, so your role is to understand what it is about and to find a way to deal with it.

WISE WORDS FROM REAL PRACTITIONERS

Reactions to change may be linked to history rather than the change itself.

However, one thing everyone knows about change is that, when change comes, people resist. So if one particular stakeholder wants to misbehave because of some historic issue that they have, that is not resistance – it is misbehaviour. People are entitled to resist change to a degree, but organisational managers have a right and a duty to deal with inappropriate behaviour according to the organisation's policies and procedures.

'I like to resist'

This last level is the rotten core of the onion. It is extremely rare in well-run organisations, but it is a real response for some people. Due to failings in their upbringing, awful experiences or some other psychological reason, some people seem to be wired to react against the smallest impulse. Good organisations can spot this in the recruitment process and, if they don't, will deal with its implications swiftly. Consequently, people like this rarely enter the best organisations and are swiftly removed if they do. But if you encounter this, once again, it is not a project issue and needs to be dealt with through other channels.

How to use the onion model

When you encounter resistance, listen carefully to what your stakeholder says and how they say it to interpret from which level the resistance is coming. It is important to always respond to the resistance at the level at which it is expressed. You may think that something deeper is going on, but there are two good reasons why you should always start with what your stakeholder actually says: first, it is just plain respectful to take people at their word; and, second, there may well be something deeper going on, but this does not mean that, for instance, they don't really understand why we need to change. And, if you don't address that concern properly, you will never properly address their resistance.

So, address the resistance as effectively as you can and, if you are not making headway, try a different tack. If you have done everything you can at one level, but you are still encountering resistance, then you can properly presume that something deeper is going on. Now, peel the onion one layer at a time and address the next layer of resistance. Keep going until you exhaust the resistance by dealing with all of the issues or you get to a rotten core.

Specific problems

We have looked at a number of forms of resistance, including the four factors that pre-dispose some people to resist more than others. Let's look at a few specific stakeholder reactions.

Objections

Objections come in all shapes and sizes and can be based on sound reasoning or spurious evidence. The simple approach to this (but remember: simple is not necessarily easy) is to 'empty the hopper'. Calmly, patiently and respectfully elicit each objection and deal with it, then elicit the next one. Keep going until there are no more objections. If the objections are disruptive, deal with the disruptive behaviour firmly and politely, and ask the stakeholder for a separate meeting. For example, objections may come during meetings or as arguments. The objections themselves may take a wide range of forms – demands for more detail, more time or more resources, assertions about viability, practicality or morality, challenges to your data, your methodology or your analysis – and they may be in the form of confrontation, silence or false compliance.

Objections may come from the microscope or the telescope. In general, 'microscope objections' are easier to deal with. These focus on tiny details and specific concerns. Whilst exhausting to deal with and maybe seeming petty to you, the reality for the stakeholder is probably a genuine desire to have their concerns addressed and, if you can do so and remain respectful, you will probably succeed in persuading this stakeholder. If one of their concerns turns out to be legitimate, accept it and make a commitment to let them know how you deal with it. Better still, enlist their support in doing so.

'Telescope objections' are harder to address because they are not specific and are often so broad that you cannot get your arms around them at all. Look out for generalisations and assertions that are based on a false premise, but take care how you challenge them. Having their objections heard and acknowledged is usually more important to these stakeholders than having them answered. Once again, however, there is a possibility that your stakeholder has identified a real and fundamental issue. You have been too caught up in the detail to see the wider context. A stakeholder who can do this is doing you a big favour.

False compliance

Some stakeholders will fear the consequences of being seen to resist. They look like they are committed, even enthusiastic supporters of the initiative, but they are far from it. It can be tempting to capitalise on their compliance and do nothing, but this is a poor strategy. They may later come to regret their compliance with a change they don't like and may become more dangerous opponents down the line. Alternatively, fooling themselves, they may set up a clash between their conscious actions and unconscious feelings, leading to stress, self-sabotage or disruptive behaviours. If you pay close attention, you can often spot signs that their support is not genuine. When you do, make the time to speak with them frankly, inviting concerns and criticism, which you can then deal with in the open.

W I S E   W O R D S   F R O M   R E A L   P R A C T I T I O N E R S

Just because someone is quiet, it does not mean that they agree – you have to go and solicit their feedback.

Myopia

Sometimes one of your stakeholders cannot see the wood for the trees. What is obvious to you does not register with them, perhaps because their range of experiences does not open them up to the pressures or opportunities your initiative is responding to. This may be an inability or unwillingness to evaluate what is before them, described by Oreg as cognitive rigidity, or it may be fear to look into the unknown, resulting in looking away, as a child does during the scary part of a film. They may simply not have the experience with which to understand what is going on. You need to create opportunities for this stakeholder to see the evidence in different ways. The final recourse is some kind of dramatic demonstration in which they cannot avoid facing up to reality.

Playing games

Some stakeholders will not be straight about their opposition – or their support. They would rather use your project as another opportunity to play politics. You have three primary strategies available to you: you can either engage them yourself, and try to build a genuine alliance, or you can look to a powerful supporter to do so on your behalf. One thing you must not do is succumb to the third strategy of getting drawn into their games. They are probably very good at it and just catching you in the web is a win for them. This means that confronting the game player head-on is unlikely to be successful and may play into their hands. There may be no winning strategy for you at all, so the third option is a strategy of not engaging. In the presence of a game player, you need powerful allies, because the game is what is important to them, not supporting your initiative or opposing it.

Sabotage

Deliberate sabotage can feel even worse, but at least the hostilities are open – unless the saboteur assumes the cloak of anonymity. Open sabotage includes constant fault-finding and blaming, missing meetings, deadlines or deliverables, or delaying responses, approvals or the release of resources. More covert forms of sabotage include poaching your people or snaffling the resources or materials that your team need, promoting or even starting a competing project, putting in false reports or starting malicious rumours, or quietly undermining your project, authority or relationships behind your back. It is not unheard of for prototypes to be damaged.

Positive engagement from the start is the best way to prevent sabotage, but if you encounter sabotage, then recognise the behaviour for what it is: bullying. If the saboteur were confident of their ground, they would confront you directly with objections. The way to deal with a bully is to be assertive with them: name the behaviour, be clear that it is unacceptable and stand up to them calmly, courteously and confidently. Bullies are cowards and, especially if you can muster some conspicuous support, they will almost certainly back down.

Losing momentum

Sometimes you will feel you have lost momentum and don't know how to regain the initiative with your stakeholders. If simply resuming the dialogue is not enough, here are three strategies to help you regain the initiative:

- Let them know your concerns and ask your stakeholders what they think will help generate progress.
- Create a big event, with a dramatic impact, to re-energise the process and get people talking. Think this through carefully: what do you want your stakeholders to be saying? Design your event around the reaction you want.
- Confront your stakeholders with a brutal truth. Often this involves exposing them to other stakeholders who are scared of the changes

you are addressing and whom you know will act if you and your other stakeholders will not. For many commercial organisations, this means exposing your staff to their customers so that they can hear first-hand why your programme is necessary.

Conflict

Although unpleasant, resistance can escalate into real conflict, which we considered in Chapter 5 (page 133). This is often triggered by the need to deliver a tough message, which is then received badly. If you can handle tough messages well, you will limit the likelihood of escalation. There are six steps to follow.

Provocation is not the same as angering someone. You need a strong relationship before you can provoke effectively.

Giving tough messages

Step 1: preparation

Before confronting a stakeholder with a tough message, first determine whether confrontation is the right approach and, if it is, how you will best do this. Do your research on them and develop your arguments, and then plan out your conversation and your fall-back positions. Think about what the issue is for them and the baggage each of you will bring to the conversation. Above all, know the outcome that you are looking for. If you can, discuss this with a close and trusted colleague, and then rehearse it all in your mind a few times.

Step 2: create safety

Deliver your message somewhere private and assure the stakeholder of the confidentiality of the situation. However, if you need to, you might want to invite an observer to attend. Start the meeting with a confident introduction to what it is about and first and foremost establish a tone of respect. If you need to, make provision for note-taking.

Step 3: deliver your message

Be clear and concise. Explain the why of what you are saying, but avoid being defensive. Acknowledge your and their discomfort. Don't be so fast that you come across as blunt, but also don't beat about the bush or use euphemisms – neither is respectful.

Step 4: pause

Allow your stakeholder to collect their thoughts and process what you have said. They may respond rationally or emotionally – accept their response for what it is and listen intently without interruption. Do not try to correct them or defend yourself while they are speaking.

Step 5: invite a dialogue

It is rarely the case that there is no scope for a dialogue, so normally you would invite them to engage in a dialogue, sharing perceptions, feeling and facts, with the intention of finding mutual ground and a way forward. Continue the dialogue for as long as you need to.

Step 6: next steps

End the process by summarising next steps, whether they are a process, support or a chance to reflect and then come back together. Separate with appropriate courtesies, but avoid over-playing it; they may feel bruised and battered and may not welcome bonhomie at this stage.

WISE WORDS FROM REAL PRACTITIONERS

Take care when relationships get too strong – they may make it easier to have the tough conversations, but the strength of your relationship may inhibit your willingness to have that conversation.

Conflict and disputes

It is beyond the scope of this book to deal further with conflict and disputes, because here, true influence breaks down. You will need to be mindful of a whole array of factors, not least of which will be how to manage the communication of what is going on to other stakeholders so that you can maintain the reputation of your project, your team and yourself, whilst not

All-out Hostility

Litigation

Disciplinary action

Arbitration

Mediation

Facilitated conversation

Talking and listening

A quiet chat

Minimal Intervention

Ignore the issue

FIGURE 7.2 / **Escalation of conflict**

attacking that of the stakeholder concerned. Figure 7.2 above shows the escalation of conflict modes that can happen during large projects, ranging from minimal intervention to nuclear warfare.

You will find a lot more tips, tricks and tools for handling resistance and conflict in a handy pocket-sized format in my book *The Handling Resistance Pocketbook*.

Your Influence Agenda: Campaign Planning

The practitioner worked on a network infrastructure roll-out for a government department. It was of high value to both the provider and the customer, involving renewal of network infrastructure and technology at over 1,000 UK sites, and was programmed to last nearly two years.

As a roll-out project, the team were doing the same thing many times, but each instance was highly dependent upon many different conditions being satisfied correctly. This made a conceptually simple project into a highly complicated one. Many of these conditions were legal or regulated agreements, and each instance had to comply with many different formal standards.

Therefore, the critical stakeholder requirement was a shared understanding of all the data, dependencies and techni-cal requirements. Connection to the new technology had to incorporate pre-existing services linked to old infrastructure. As a result, the timing of testing and cut-over was a key factor. A formal notice period was required for any planned outages of service so that operational teams could prepare for any disrup-tion that might have resulted.

The team's emphasis was on maintaining formal communica-tion channels and making them as effective as possible. Regular meetings took place at all levels from senior management through to operational teams, both within the supplier organisation and between the supplier's project team and the customer's senior and operational managers.

At one point, the team decided to advance progress towards the end of an accounting period and set ambitious completion targets. They took calculated risks to push their schedule and were rewarded by a significant rise in the number of completions (more than balancing out the slight increase in failure rates). This was widely celebrated. However, the project manager had not foreseen the stakeholder response at the start of the succeeding period, when a dip in completions as a result of accelerating completions that would have naturally fallen into the next period led to a perception among stakeholders that the project had stalled. The team had failed to prepare stakeholders for the planned dip in completions, leading to avoidable adverse perceptions.

Some local authorities have a 13-week lead time before they can notify statutory undertakers of a date when they can close the road for laying underground services. While the obvious options are to wait or to find alternative solutions where possible, the team re-framed these stakeholders from being perceived as blockers to progress to being seen as a planning constraint.

Having identified stakeholders with a major influence on timing, the team planned accordingly, putting in applications well in advance of needing them resolved. Some stakeholders have a primary influence on your project planning and the timing of your master programme.

In Chapter 4, we focused on developing a strategy and messages for each stakeholder. This chapter is different – it looks at creating a campaign plan across the full range of your stakeholders. We do this primarily to create a coherent approach, not just in the integrity of the messages we will deliver, but in managing the timing, the prioritisation and allocation of resources, and the responsiveness of our campaign.

A stakeholder engagement campaign

Your stakeholder engagement campaign needs a coherent plan that sets out how you will manage each of your stakeholder relationships and what you aim to achieve with each of them in terms of the strength and orientation of the relationship, and the perceptions and behaviours of the stakeholder. As well as goals and priorities, however, your stakeholder engagement campaign needs action plans for each stakeholder.

Chapters 2 and 3 gave you the tools you need to get started, inventorying your stakeholders and your relationships with them, to analyse those stakeholders and to identify which will be strategically most important. These allowed you to complete the first two sections of a stakeholder register. Your stakeholder engagement plan is section 3 of your stakeholder register.

Whilst different types of project and programme will need different plan structures, your plans will incorporate a common set of components.

Components of your campaign plan

The stakeholders

Your campaign plan will start from your list of stakeholders and your analysis of each of them. This will allow you to segment stakeholders into different groupings to simplify your planning process. The obvious groupings, which you may often use, is based on prioritisation, determining the amount of effort and the urgency you will apply to different sets of stakeholders. Some stakeholders may be important enough to you to track and manage individually.

The levers

Your plan needs to identify what levers you will use to persuade or motivate stakeholders to engage, act or change their behaviours. Chapters 4, 5 and 6 covered this extensively. A simple fourfold categorisation of motivating levers (see Figure 5.3 in Chapter 5) is as follows:

1. *Intrinsic motivation*
   This is the most powerful and is designed to appeal directly to the stakeholder by making the actions you want to motivate desirable to them.

2. *Social motivation*

   This is also powerful, engaging your stakeholder's social nature to motivate through relationships, obligations, conformity or the need to protect their reputation or status.

3. *Extrinsic motivation*

   Perhaps the weakest motivations are those linked to rewards, pleasures and the threat of withdrawing them. These should only be used as a last resort.

4. *Foundational motivation*

   Safety and security are fundamental, so appealing to them is powerful. But, ultimately, it is a bullying tactic that I recommend you leave well alone.

The message and the medium

Chapter 4 focused on the message and the means by which you will deliver it. In a complex programme, each stakeholder may need to receive multiple messages and you will need a number of different media to ensure that the messages have the greatest chance of getting through.

The timing

An important part of your campaign plan is the sequencing of messages to avoid confusion, breaking complex messages into smaller chunks so that sophisticated details can build upon earlier, simpler messages. Timing is also critical and often needs to be coordinated with the master schedule for your project or change programme so that key messages arrive in synchronisation with planned events. Some messages will be advisory and will need to be communicated in advance of events – and, indeed, there may be minimum notification periods to consider. Others will be scheduled to follow closely after events, such as celebratory messages.

The responsibilities

How will you actually get the messages across? You need to allocate responsibilities to specific people or groups, possibly setting out explicit roles and capability requirements. Capabilities may be expressed in terms of personal skills and characteristics, and physical resources that communicators can draw upon. A serious mistake is to allow overlapping responsibilities that can lead to messages becoming confused when they are communicated twice, in subtly different ways. We avoid this from happening in high-pressure crisis situations by appointing a single spokesperson as the only person empowered to speak on behalf of the organisation or project.

The feedback

Engagement is a two-way process. You cannot hope to influence your stakeholders unless you can gauge their response to your messages. So your plan needs a mechanism for gathering and evaluating feedback. This will allow you to test the efficacy of your communication and you can also use it as a basis for improving your plans for the next stage. Some stakeholders will happily provide you with all of the feedback you need; others will be reticent, so invite feedback, make it easy to give and take an active role in gathering it. Listening is one of your most valuable skills.

Treat feedback as a gift, regardless of how uncomfortable its implications are. Bad news can always be the basis of a new plan, unless you choose to ignore it. This is where personal resilience is an important characteristic for a stakeholder engagement professional.

The policies

Your organisation – or even a broad programme infrastructure – may impose policies upon you that need to be factored into your stakeholder engagement plan. These could include who may speak with certain stakeholders, how information is recorded or the use of certain jargon or terminology. This will almost certainly be the case at times of crisis and when dealing with the media.

The monitor, control and review cycle

The last part of your stakeholder engagement plan will cover how you propose to monitor the results of your stakeholder engagement, the mechanisms for adjusting the process and keeping it on track, and the process you will use to review your team's performance and the effectiveness of your processes against your engagement goals and targets.

Stakeholder engagement plan template

The following template sets out a basic stakeholder engagement plan. You can download a sample stakeholder engagement plan template from www.theinfluenceagenda.co.uk.

Template 8.1   Stakeholder engagement plan

Section 1: Control Data			
Project:			
Reference No:		Document No & Version:	
Project Manager:		Project Sponsor:	

Version Control			
Issue No	Date	Author	Description

Policies Relevant to Stakeholder Engagement		
Reference	Policy	Applicability

Section 2: Stakeholders				
	Analysis			
Stakeholder	Impact	Attitude	Interests	Narrative

Section 3: Stakeholder Strategy	
Stakeholder	Strategy (Levers and Approaches)

Section 4: Stakeholder Messages				
Stakeholder	Message	Medium	Timing	Responsible
	1 2 3			
	1 2 3			

(continued)

Template 8.1　Continued

Feedback Mechanisms	
Stakeholder	Feedback Mechanisms
	1
	2
	3
	1
	2
	3

Section 5: Campaign Management
Campaign Monitoring and Control
Campaign Review

Strategic posture

A simple tool like a proximity map (see Appendix 3) or an analysis of power, impact, influence or interest can yield an effective prioritisation of your stakeholders. Different levels of stakeholder will merit a different level of strategic priority. For example, you might identify three tiers of stakeholder priority, as illustrated below:

1. *Tier one stakeholders* are customers, shareholders, directors, senior managers and key managerial and operational staff.
2. *Tier two stakeholders* are statutory, regulatory and compliance stakeholders to whom legislation or policy gives you a responsibility.
3. *Tier three stakeholders* are all other stakeholders. These have interests that you must engage with for reasons of ethics, equity or pragmatism.

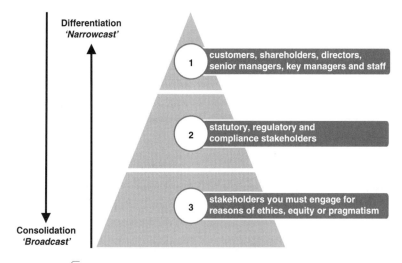

FIGURE 8.1 / Stakeholder prioritisation

In this figure, we show how the smaller numbers of higher-priority stakeholders are treated with greater differentiation – each receiving a more tailored strategy. The lower-tier stakeholders are increasingly consolidated into engagement processes that treat them as more homogeneous groupings. There will still be some segmentation at these levels, but the 'chunk-size' will be greater.

For each stakeholder or stakeholder group, determine your strategic posture, which will lie on a scale from highly accommodating to aggressively coercive (as if you would!). Table 8.1 gives an example of what a simple scale might look like.

Table 8.1   Strategic postures

Focus	Posture	
Focus on stakeholders	1. Accommodating	Prepared to make substantial concessions to the stakeholder to achieve the core intention.
	2. Collaborating	Prepared to work together with the stakeholder to achieve mutually beneficial outcomes.
	3. Consulting	Consulting actively and open to compromise.
Neutral	4. Informing	Open sharing of information.
Focus on organisation or project objectives	5. Promotional	Use of promotional and persuasive tactics to influence stakeholders positively.
	6. Defensive	Resisting compromise and providing strong counter-arguments to stakeholders' perceptions.
	7. Assertive	Prepared to fight hard to optimise the position of the project or organisation. Extent of tactics dictated by ethics and long-term pragmatism.

You can use these different strategic postures to create a stakeholder strategy chart that maps your stakeholders against your chosen set of strategic postures.

	Stakeholder 1	Stakeholder 2	Stakeholder 3
Accommodating			
Collaborating		Key stakeholder with significant power	
Consulting	Important stakeholder with valuable insights		
Informing			
Promotional			
Defensive			Low-impact stakeholder with narrow interests
Assertive			

FIGURE 8.2   Stakeholder strategy chart

The pattern that emerges in this chart will reflect your interpretation of the prevailing culture in your organisation. For example, an open and altruistic culture would generate a substantial weight of strategies at the top of the chart, whilst a self-interested and coercive culture would show the opposite, with most strategic postures lying in the lower half. An obsequious hierarchical culture, however, will show a lot of top-half postures against senior level high-power stakeholders with other stakeholders allocated lower-half postures.

We can extend this approach to find a wide range of strategic postures based on the two dimensions of level of engagement and level of collaboration. In Figure 8.3 below, the vertical axis measures the degree of collaboration, from actively working against your stakeholders, or 'competing', to working with your stakeholders, or 'collaborating'. The horizontal axis measures the extent to which you engage with your stakeholders, from actively withdrawing from them, or 'avoiding', to consciously getting involved with them, or 'engaging'.

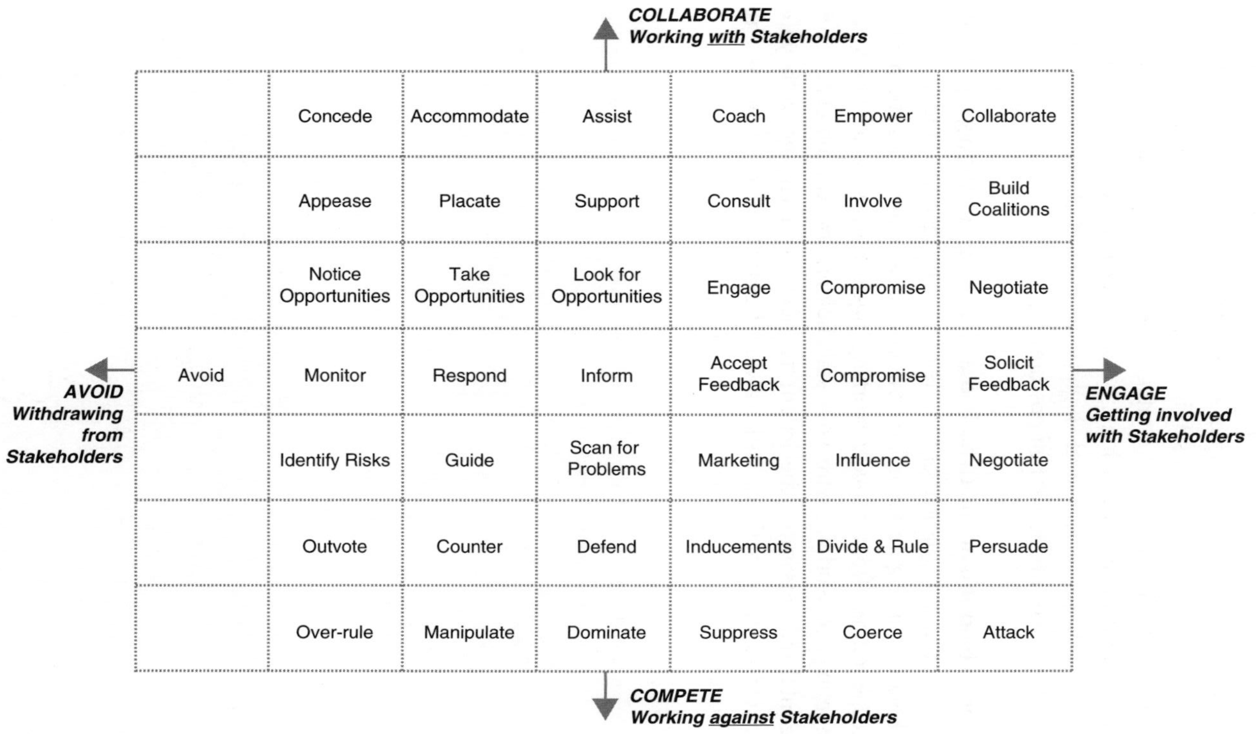

The matrix shows stakeholder engagement strategies arranged in a grid, with axes labeled:
- **COLLABORATE** *Working with Stakeholders* (top-left)
- **ENGAGE** *Getting involved with Stakeholders* (right)
- **COMPETE** *Working against Stakeholders* (bottom-right)
- **AVOID** *Withdrawing from Stakeholders* (bottom-left)

	Concede	Accommodate	Assist	Coach	Empower	Collaborate
	Appease	Placate	Support	Consult	Involve	Build Coalitions
	Notice Opportunities	Take Opportunities	Look for Opportunities	Engage	Compromise	Negotiate
Avoid	Monitor	Respond	Inform	Accept Feedback	Compromise	Solicit Feedback
	Identify Risks	Guide	Scan for Problems	Marketing	Influence	Negotiate
	Outvote	Counter	Defend	Inducements	Divide & Rule	Persuade
	Over-rule	Manipulate	Dominate	Suppress	Coerce	Attack

FIGURE 8.3 / **Stakeholder engagement strategies**

The long game

While we are talking about strategic posture, there is nothing more strategic than the 'long game' of relationships: building up strategic relationships with the leaders and apex stakeholders of tomorrow. This is what ultimately can make you into an apex stakeholder yourself. It is tempting to de-prioritise junior staff, but remember Stakeholder Rule Number 6: *tomorrow's leaders are today's juniors*.

Don't just cast your eyes upwards when relationship building. The challenge, of course, is that this is not a symmetric relationship: *all* of tomorrow's leaders are today's juniors, but few of today's juniors are tomorrow's leaders. This kind of relationship building will always be a portfolio investment: sow many seeds, knowing that a few will germinate and grow strong. This is a particularly important aspect of relationship building if you are in the early stages of your career. The close relationships you build with your peers today will become the high-level stakeholder relationships that will serve you well as your career matures.

WISE WORDS FROM REAL PRACTITIONERS

Don't under-estimate the goodwill and support you can build up with your relationships. Your efforts can be re-paid when stakeholders come out of the woodwork with offers of help when you most need them.

Team effort

Good stakeholder engagement is a team effort. On smaller change initiatives and projects, there will be no dedicated stakeholder engagement manager, so the role will be picked up either by the project or programme manager or by one of your team. When the role is fulfilled by a dedicated professional, they will still not have the capacity to do all of the work themselves of engaging with every stakeholder – their role is about strategy and planning, coordination and participating in engagement with key stakeholders. Everyone from the sponsor and the project board members to the junior team members has a part to play.

Each team member can build their own networks and create their own opportunities to influence and enrol stakeholders. The role of the stakeholder engagement manager is to coordinate efforts, to avoid overkill or gaps being left, to support team members with scheduling, support and guidance, and maybe to provide training or coaching on how the team members can be effective in building and strengthening relationships and in deploying persuasive tactics. A simple relationship map can show how your team members are connected to your stakeholders.

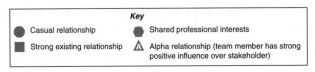

	Team member A	Team member B	Team member C
Stakeholder 1		⬡ IEE membership	
Stakeholder 2	⬡ CIPD membership		
Stakeholder 3			⬛ Worked together in previous company
Stakeholder 4		●	
Stakeholder 5	⬛A Has provided advice several times	●	
Stakeholder 6			

FIGURE 8.4 **Team-member relationship map**

Team members can be deployed in a wide range of ways: informally speaking with contacts, involvement in hosting consultation meetings, performing a facilitation role in pilot events, writing contributions to newsletters or posting on social media.

Roles and responsibilities

It makes good sense to formalise the roles and responsibilities of active participants in projects and change programmes, not just for the sake of good governance, but also to support effective management and job performance monitoring. The descriptions in Table 8.2 below are typical of those relating to the stakeholder engagement aspect of team members' roles and responsibilities. What is important is that the project or programme manager designs and agrees with their sponsor a consistent set of roles and responsibilities that can be published and briefed to all participants.

Table 8.2   Stakeholder engagement roles and responsibilities

Sponsor, executive or senior responsible owner	Visible, consistent leadership of the project/programme.
	Engage with senior-level stakeholders within and outside of the organisation.
	Actively promote the programme/project at all opportunities.
	Resolve highest-level stakeholder issues.
	Provide guidance and support to the project or programme manager.
Programme board member or other senior executives with sponsoring or governance roles	Engage with senior-level stakeholders within and outside of the organisation.
	Actively promote the programme/project at all opportunities.
	Review and approve stakeholder engagement plan.
	Provide oversight of all strategic-level stakeholder communication and sign-off for sensitive initiatives.
	Resolve highest-level stakeholder issues.
Steering group member or other senior executives with a role in designing outcomes	Engage with senior-level stakeholders within and outside of the organisation.
	Actively promote the programme/project at all opportunities.
	Advise on communication strategies and tactics for specific stakeholders and groupings.
Project or programme manager	Lead all stakeholder analysis, planning and engagement activities.
	Engage with senior- and mid-level stakeholders within and outside of the organisation.
	Actively promote the programme/project at all opportunities.
	Provide guidance and support to other team members.
Stakeholder engagement manager	Identify and analyse stakeholders.
	Build stakeholder engagement plan.
	Design, manage, coordinate and evaluate all stakeholder engagement activities.
	Engage with senior- and mid-level stakeholders within and outside of the organisation.
	Provide guidance and support to other team members, including the project/programme manager.
Integration or business change manager and team	Engage with operational stakeholders within and outside of the organisation.
	Inform project/programme manager or stakeholder engagement manager of concerns raised by operational stakeholders.
	Actively promote the programme/project at all opportunities.

(continued)

Table 8.2   Continued

Programme management office or project support office members	Support project/programme manager and stakeholder engagement manager in planning, tracking and evaluating all stakeholder engagement activities. Maintain all stakeholder registers and planning tools (including revisions, version control and data protection). Actively promote the programme/project at all opportunities.
Project team members	Actively promote the programme/project at all opportunities. Support stakeholder engagement activities as required.

Building your campaign plan

This section contains a range of useful campaign planning tools for you to adapt to your own needs. You can download templates for each of them from www.theinfluenceagenda.co.uk.

Communication plan

Perhaps the most commonly used stakeholder planning tool of all is a basic communication plan. At its simplest, it is a table showing, for each stakeholder, the elements of the plan for communicating with them, as illustrated in Template 8.2 below.

Template 8.2   Basic stakeholder communication plan

	Stakeholder 1	Stakeholder 2	Stakeholder 3
Objectives			
Message: what to communicate			
Tone			
Medium: method of communication			
Feedback: how will we test understanding?			
Timing or frequency			
Person responsible			

You may want to focus your plan instead upon the communications that you put out. Template 8.3 below does this.

Template 8.3   Basic communications plan

	Communication A	Communication B	Communication C
Circulation: stakeholders who will receive it			
Nature: medium and style of the communication			
Message: information or persuasive argument			
Owner: who will design and publish the communication?			
Feedback: how will we test understanding?			
Timing or frequency			

However, for many stakeholders, these approaches can be too simple: the stakeholder will need to be engaged multiple times, with different messages, via different media and by different people. The alternative is illustrated in Template 8.4 below.

Template 8.4   Single-stakeholder communications plan

Stakeholder	
Overall stakeholder goals and objectives	

Message Schedule					
Message to communicate, tone to take and level of detail	*Medium*	*Feedback methods to attract, record, and evaluate*	*Timing*	*Person responsible*	*Budget*

In each of these, the reference to the communication tool or medium offers the widest possible scope, and Appendix 4 provides you with a vast checklist of possibilities. The question can arise as to which medium to use. The simplest approach to selection is to base it upon the strategic posture you wish to adopt. Figure 8.5 below provides an indicative selection guide.

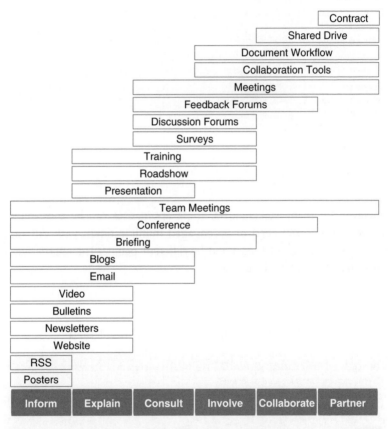

FIGURE 8.5 **Selecting a communication medium according to strategic posture**

An alternative is to choose a medium according to the nature of the message, and a simple grid is illustrated in Figure 8.6 below.

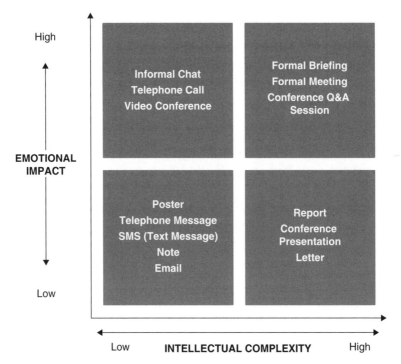

FIGURE 8.6 Selecting a communication medium according to the nature of the message

Communication approach grid

This simple tool creates a grid of all of the messages you need to get across to your stakeholders and all of the media you have available to you. At each intersection, you can place the stakeholders whom you will target with each message/medium combination and the schedule for the message. A simplified example is set out in Template 8.5 below.

Template 8.5 Communications approach grid

	Newsletter	Formal report	Briefing meeting	Conference
Progress updates	Staff and line management	Senior management		
Process design briefings		Senior management	Line management	
New product schedule	Customers			
Pre-launch briefing		Senior management	Staff and line management	Customers

Impression plan

The purpose of an impression plan is focus on the messages you will give to create a desired impression or perception. It lists all of the available communication means, often harnessing pre-existing channels, along the top of a grid. You can then use it to document the elements of your impression plan for each: the current impressions and perceptions, the impression you want to convey, the actions to take, start and finish dates, allocation of responsibility and the budget.

Template 8.6   Impression plan

	Corporate annual report	Office area posters	Bi-monthly staff newsletter
Current impression			
Desired impression			
Actions to take	1 2	1 2	1 2
Start date/completion date			
Person responsible			
Budget allocation			

Message calendar

What could be simpler than a calendar with the key messages for the day or week in each box? These are used in political campaigns, where messages are colour-coded by theme, such as red for domestic, blue for economy, purple for foreign and green for environment. Template 8.7 below shows a simple example of a message calendar.

Template 8.7   Message calendar

	Week 1	Week 2	Week 3
Theme			
Messages	1 2 3		
Notes			
Announcements			
Meetings			
Events			
Newsletters			
Social media			

Progression plan

Projects have distinct stages and change initiatives move people through stages of a response cycle from denial, through emotional responses like anger or fear, to active resistance, to an engagement with the consequences, to acceptance and finally (if things go well) to a commitment to the change. We use progression plans to chart out the key messages that we need to communicate at each stage. Template 8.8 below is a simple progression plan based on familiar project stages.

Template 8.8   Progression plan – project stages

Project stage	Crucial stakeholders	Key messages
Definition		
Planning		
Procurement		
Prototyping		
Delivery		
Testing		
Closure		
Post-project review		

This second sample is the equivalent approach, this time for an internal change programme. It is targeted at one stakeholder group: the staff. The stages are those of a standard change programme and the interventions and messages need to be designed to consolidate the bulk of the staff at each stage of the change cycle, and then prepare them to move on.

Template 8.9   Progression plan – change programme

Change cycle stage		Messages to deliver	Interventions by which to deliver the messages
Unfreezing	Move out of *denial*		
	Consolidate in *recognition*		
	Move towards *resistance*		
Changing	Handle *resistance*		
	Move towards *exploration*		
	Consolidate *exploration*		
	Move towards *acceptance*		
Re-freezing	Consolidate *acceptance*		
	Move towards *commitment*		
	Consolidate *commitment*		

Working with the media

Working with the media is a specialised area and the best advice is to put it in the hands of professionals who have appropriate public relations experience in your sector. The principal media to consider are broadcast, print and web media.

Broadcast media

This is radio and television. Both are looking for topical news stories or engaging features that can be planned ahead. Television is also looking for strong visual contexts and telegenic people to feature, whilst radio needs confident voices and distinctive sounds to support its storytelling. For most stories, the place to start is with local channels: if the story is good enough, national networks will pick it up. So think about how to emphasise the local angle. All news is local. Preparation and rehearsal are vital, so make sure to practise making your point clearly and succinctly. Editors will want to cut and trim your contribution, so if it is already a short and perfectly formed soundbite, there is nothing they can do to cut it and thereby misrepresent you. This is why politicians so often speak in prepared soundbites. If you are going to appear on broadcast media, do consider getting media training.

If you find yourself getting interviewed, practise the SCOPE method to SCOPE each question you are asked:

Stop	Pause. Don't jump in with an answer, but take a moment to create some tension for the audience and impact for you.
Clarify	If the question is not 100 per cent clear to you, ask for clarification or re-state the question in your terms to be sure you answer the right question.
Options	Mentally go through the ways you could answer the question. With good preparation, it will be close to one you have practised.
Proceed	Give your answer, and answer only the question asked. Look at your interviewer or into the camera (depending on the camera angle) and sit or stand upright and still. Don't offer uninvited speculation, don't tell the interviewer what they should have asked you and don't explain your thought processes. These are the keys to being believable.
Evaluate	Ask politely if the interviewer has a follow-up question. Don't ask if your answer was OK, however – that would suggest that you have doubts about it.

Print media

This is primarily the press and magazines. Once again, local press and trade or professional magazines are an easier target than the national press or newsagent shelf magazines. Attract attention with an arresting press release and make sure your notes do much of the work for a busy journalist. Consider getting high-quality photos to offer for publication and be prepared to make yourself available at short notice for interviews and photo shoots. Many magazines and local papers need copy, so offering articles can sometimes bear fruit. Magazines have long lead times – up to three months for the big glossies – so plan this into your campaign.

You can download a sample press release template from www.theinfluence agenda.co.uk.

Web media

Whether it is the web equivalents of television or press media (like the Huffington Post) or a narrow interest blogger, the web can be a great way to communicate a good story. It is thirsty for content, persists for longer and allows far more content in the form of social media and website links, photos and video. Don't be put off by the amateur nature of much of the web; some sites have massive readerships and their editors have become as powerful as traditional editors – sometimes with similar levels of skill and ruthlessness in choosing and editing articles.

Consolidate your web media campaign with your social media campaign. As with print media, the web loves images, so prepare copies of your pictures in web-size format. The web also loves video, so consider preparing simple video clips of one to three minutes.

WISE WORDS FROM REAL PRACTITIONERS

We often tend to create a stakeholder plan when we hit a problem. We try to understand where our problem fits into the universe of people. Instead, make your plan up-front, based on an understanding of your universe of people.

9

Making it Work: Campaign Management

I have often felt that the secret to success in any endeavour is 'intelligent persistence' – the quality of keeping working at something important, but in a way that constantly reviews the efficacy of what you are doing and makes adjustments accordingly. This is what campaign management is all about.

Just like polishing a pebble at the bed of a stream, building relationships and changing attitudes takes time. Unlike the pebble, though, what has one effect on people today may have a very different effect on them tomorrow, so you need to be constantly evaluating what you are doing so that you can make changes to stay in control of the situation. This is the 'monitor and control loop': act – observe – interpret – intervene.

In this chapter, we will look at how you can apply this general principle to managing stakeholder engagement and then take it three steps further, to evaluate the performance of your campaign, to learn from it and then, ultimately, to grow and embed a positive stakeholder engagement culture.

Monitor

In Chapter 1, we introduced a simple process for stakeholder engagement.

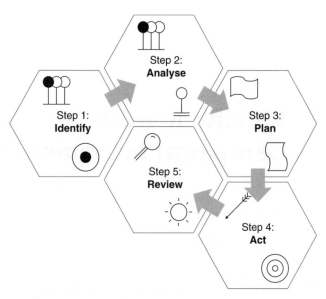

FIGURE 1.4 The stakeholder engagement process

It would be easy to represent the sequence in a simple, linear way, but the review step is, and should be, right at the heart of the process. We will see why in the next section when we look at how to maintain control of the process. But the review step consists of two processes: monitor and control.

The purpose of monitoring is to become aware of your performance so that you can control what you are doing. The more effectively you can gather and understand the data about your progress and how it compares with your plan, the more effectively you will be able to intervene to optimise your next move.

Monitor progress both formally and informally. Informally, chat with your project colleagues about their experiences. Formally, assess the communications that you have made and evaluate the feedback you have had in response. Compare the timings of your actions against your plan, examine your expenditure and compare it with your budget, and review the performance of your colleagues. It is easy to leave this kind of monitoring until you reach your once-a-month reporting cycle, but stakeholder engagement is far too important to be considered as just another set of data to be incorporated into a formal report. The more active your engagement process is, the more frequently you need to be monitoring what is happening and how effective it is. And if you are not engaging actively enough, your project will run into difficulties, so one of the questions you must constantly be asking yourself is: 'Are we doing enough?' Are there stakeholders with whom you could and should be engaging more often and with more commitment?

An inward-looking change or project manager is unlikely to be completely successful. Also look outwards to spot changes in your environment that can affect what you are doing. Speaking with stakeholders will help you with this. Form a stakeholder engagement management perspective; look at how these changes are affecting stakeholders' attitudes, power and relationships. What do these mean for your plans?

There are many sources of change to be aware of, but eight of the most common can easily be remembered using the acronym 'SPECTRES' mentioned in Chapter 2. SPECTRES should remind you to look for changes in the following:

- *Society* – the social changes that drive many organisational plans and may be responsible for the changes you are working to create.
- *Politics* – not just national and local politics, but organisational politics too. When two stakeholders are discussing your project, that's politics!
- *Economics* – the macroeconomy and also project economics and pressures on your budget.
- *Competitive* – these days, even not-for-profit and public sector organisations operate in a competitive environment.
- *Technology* – technology changes alarmingly quickly, not just with the rate of introduction of new technology, but also in the pace of adoption. Internet technologies have transformed aspects of society and of stakeholder engagement.
- *Regulation* – legislation and regulation change frequently and can alter the rules by which you need to play. Most, however, have a clear lead time, making this easier to plan for than some of the other pressures.
- *Environment* – one of the hot buttons of the twenty-first century, but remember that the environment that many people care most about is their immediate environment: the light levels on the factory floor, the cleanliness of the warehouse or the air quality in the office.
- *Security* – issues of physical security have been overtaken in organisational life by concerns about privacy and data security. This is an arena that will see much change in the years following the publication of this book.

All of these changes will have profound effects on your priorities: which stakeholders are most crucial, what messages you need to put out, how to frame those messages and what tone to adopt, and timing. Therefore, use your assessment of your effectiveness and the changes that have happened to revise your stakeholder maps and review your plans. If necessary, take the time to start afresh and create a new strategy. It is better to abandon an out-of-date, failing strategy and accept a short delay while you craft a new one than to continue to pursue it, knowing that it will be ultimately futile. When in a hole, stop digging.

Control

The control process depends upon what your monitoring shows up. There are three alternative versions of the monitor and control loop, which we could characterise as follows:

1. *The maintenance cycle*: tweaks to stay in control when events are going broadly according to plan.
2. *The persuasion cycle*: to increase your level of control if you are not making the headway you would wish to make.
3. *The response cycle*: to re-assert control if you are in danger of losing it or if you already have lost control.

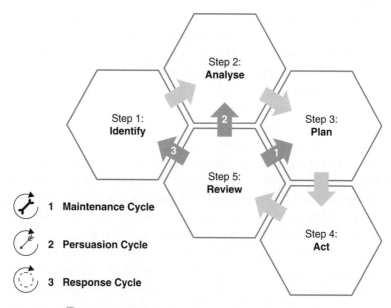

FIGURE 9.1   The maintenance, persuasion and response cycles

The maintenance cycle

If you are making the progress you need to make, your plans are working and external events have not changed circumstances materially, then you will feel in control of your engagement process. You need to do no more in this situation than maintain the currency of your plan, making tweaks and adjustments as necessary, to react to the details of what is happening. The plan-act-review maintenance cycle looks very much like the fundamental control cycle first introduced by Walter Shewhart and popularised by W. Edwards Deming, the 'Shewhart Cycle' of plan-do-study-act, also known as the 'Deming Cycle'. The review stage and the updating of your plan is Shewhart's 'study' step.

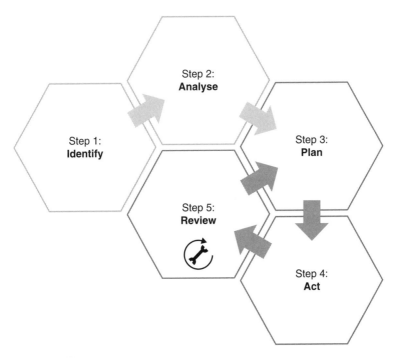

FIGURE 9.2 / The maintenance cycle

The persuasion cycle

If you are not making the progress you need to and have to improve your processes substantially, the persuasion cycle allows you to further

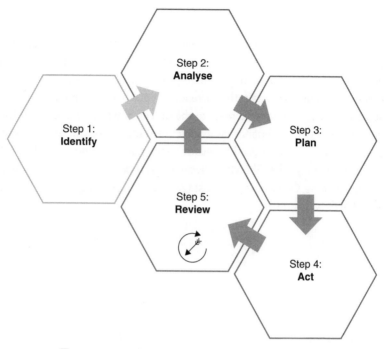

FIGURE 9.3 / The persuasion cycle

extend Shewhart's study step by re-visiting aspects of your analysis. This may be remedial – to address shortcomings in earlier work – or it may be to respond to changes in the situation or in your stakeholders' responses, attitudes or status. Don't think, by the way, that a remedial analysis necessarily means your original analysis was at fault; you had to make choices about how much investment to put into the processes and sometimes we get these decisions wrong. With further analysis, you have the basis for upgrading your plans and therefore improving your persuasion process.

The response cycle

If events change things substantially, you will need to review who your new and emerging stakeholders are before re-visiting your analysis. Potentially, this could be a full re-start of your stakeholder engagement process. More likely, however, you will start with a new stakeholder identification exercise and a critical review of your earlier analysis.

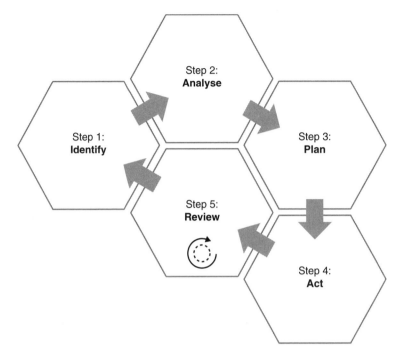

FIGURE 9.4 The response cycle

Evaluate

An important part of the review process is a periodic deep evaluation of your work – a 'stakeholder engagement audit'. The process for this follows five initial steps, with two natural continuation steps, which we will look at in the next two major sections of this chapter:

Step 1. Determine the *terms of reference* for your audit.
Step 2. Develop *evaluation criteria* against which to evaluate your performance.
Step 3. *Collect* your data.
Step 4. *Analyse* your data.
Step 5. Present your *report and recommendations*.
Follow-on steps
Step 6. *Learn* from the process so that you can improve your stakeholder engagement process.

Step 7.   Use the audit results to further *embed* stakeholder engagement into your corporate processes.

Terms of reference

There are five elements to defining your audit:

1. Its goal or purpose.
2. The success criteria – often expressed in terms of the quality standard for the analysis.
3. The deadline.
4. The resources to be deployed.
5. The scope of your study – its breadth and depth.

Questions to ask at this stage include the following:

- Why do we need to engage with stakeholders?
- Why do we want to conduct an audit and who will it be for?
- What information will be most valuable to us? If it cannot guide your decisions, it is for interest only.
- What resources are we prepared to commit to evaluating our performance?
- Who should properly be involved in the audit – and who should we exclude?
- When do we need answers? The sooner the better, in terms of taking any remedial action, but a faster result requires either more resources or compromises to the quality or scope of the review.
- How many people do we need to talk with and how will we select our sample?
- What objective data do we need?
- How can we make the audit a valuable part of our overall engagement process?
- What format should the final report take and who will receive copies of it?

Once you have clarified and agreed your terms of reference, you can start planning how you will conduct your audit. With your plan in place, your next step is to consider what is important to you in engaging with stakeholders and therefore the criteria you will audit your performance against.

The practitioner was a Senior Programme Director sent to recover a failing technology programme for a major client by the large systems delivery company that he worked for. His first step was to review senior-level relationships between the contractor's existing Programme Director and the client's board-level executive.

The Programme Director assured the reviewer that he had a good relationship with the senior stakeholder, that they met regularly (at least once a month) and had good discussions. He was the only point of contact between the provider's management team and this senior client stakeholder.

When the reviewer pushed for details of the relationship, the Programme Director conceded that the last meeting was 'a few weeks ago' and then, when pushed again, consulted his diary and found it was 11 weeks since they had last met.

'How did it go?' asked the reviewer. The response was that the Programme Director had a number of points to raise, but that they got stuck on some of the delays and various technical problems, and that he had had to leave early. On further questioning, it transpired that the discussion had become heated, the Programme Director had argued with his stakeholder to the extent that he was thrown out of the office. He had not been in touch again for 11 weeks.

The Programme Director was exhibiting what the reviewer describes as 'ostrich behaviour' – a head-in-the-sand approach that denied the reality of the situation. This situation was about honesty – with yourself. Relationships do struggle, but we need to face up to the reality of a situation gone sour and step up to the situation and deal with it professionally. The Programme Director should have prepared for and had the difficult conversation that was needed to start to re-build the relationship and deal with the project's problems.

Evaluation criteria

Your stakeholder audit needs to align with the goals, the strategy and the values of your organisation, your programme and your stakeholder engagement process, so the evaluation criteria you choose must be drawn from all of these. This strongly suggests a 'balanced scorecard' approach, where you evaluate across a range of different criteria to ensure that the work you are doing does not disproportionately focus on some of your objectives at the cost of others. To develop a balanced scorecard, you need to think about all of the objectives your stakeholder engagement process might have and cluster them into groups that represent similar concerns. The different groups must therefore be balanced according to a considered prioritisation. An example is given in Figure 9.5 below.

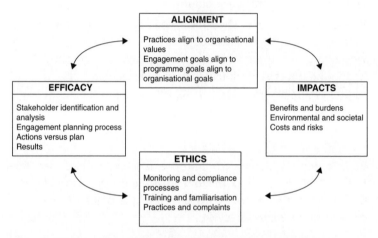

FIGURE 9.5 **Example of a balanced stakeholder engagement scorecard**

Data collection

In addition to a basic review of reports and other published material, you can gather this information in a number of ways:

- *Interviews.* The most nuanced information about perceptions of your project or the change, levels of awareness and how your engagement efforts are being received will come from extended interviews. Ideally, these will be carried out by a third party who is separate from your engagement process or, as a minimum, by someone who does not regularly engage with the stakeholder. Done well, the interview can add to awareness and improve perceptions, but you will need to take care to design it so that this positive and desirable effect does not feed directly into the results, invalidating the audit.

- *Forums and focus groups.* The halfway house between a resource-intensive personal interview and the impersonal approach of a survey is a forum or focus group, in which a facilitator creates discussion among participants and an observer records the information that the forum has been designed to elicit. Doing this well requires skill, training and some experience, so again you may want to involve a third party.
- *Polls and surveys.* It is easy to create effective surveys using web-based tools. These allow you to gather quantitative data and written perceptual data, and the tools also automate large elements of your data analysis.

Data analysis

The fundamental principle of a performance audit is that performance is measured against a baseline. Ideally, you will conduct the audit against your evaluation criteria right at the start of your project, change initiative or stakeholder engagement process to establish that baseline. Often, the single most important measure in a stakeholder audit is the attitude of your stakeholders, which, if you are engaging effectively, will improve with time. You can easily chart average attitude against time to show this trend, but this contains little information. Three other simple graphs can be used to illustrate the evolution of stakeholder attitudes in a richer way. Each adds additional information that may interest the people to whom you are reporting.

In Figure 9.6 below, each line represents the attitudes of your individual stakeholders at one point in time. If each line is higher than the previous one, you are having a positive effect on stakeholder attitudes. Individual peaks and troughs in a line represent stakeholders who are, respectively, particular supporters and critics of your activities.

Each curve in Figure 9.7 below represents the distribution of support among a large sample of stakeholders. If the sample you measure each time is the same, then the areas under each curve will be the same. As attitudes improve, you will see the peak of the curve move to the right. A tighter, narrower peak represents a more coherent 'herd attitude'. Note that it is quite possible to see two distinct peaks at each end, representing

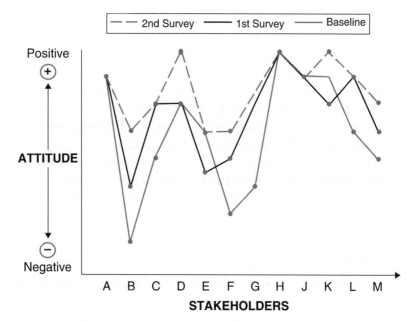

FIGURE 9.6 / Evolution of individual stakeholder attitudes

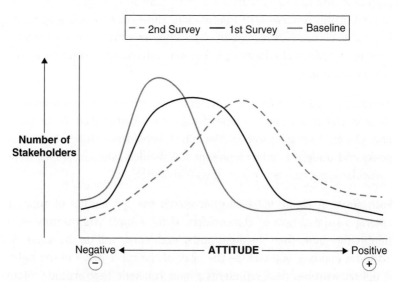

FIGURE 9.7 / Spread of stakeholder attitudes

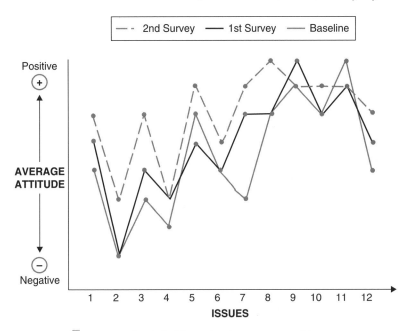

FIGURE 9.8 / Averages of stakeholder attitudes to a range of issues

a polarised stakeholder group, in which substantial numbers oppose and support you.

If you want to represent attitudes to a range of different issues (labelled 1, 2, 3, etc. in Figure 9.8 above), then you can calculate an average attitude among a stakeholder sample at each survey. Successive surveys give different lines and, once again, if a line lies above previous ones, attitudes are improving. This chart highlights which issues are of particular concern to stakeholders and which are widely supported, and also which issues have shown big changes (positive or adverse) in levels of support. What it does not show is the range of views.

These three examples are just a sample of the ways you can illustrate information about your stakeholders' perceptions.

Reporting and recommendations

You should have determined the format and content of your report as part of your terms of reference and then gathered and analysed your data to fit into it. This is not to imply that data will never contain surprises; you do need a certain flexibility in your report's structure. The most important aspects of a good report are clarity, accuracy, relevance and practicality:

- The data must be presented in a way that makes it easy for the reader to assimilate and understand.
- You must check it scrupulously for errors, because one mistake can undermine the credibility of a whole audit.
- Present only information that is relevant – interesting facts that will not influence decisions or future actions can be saved for social anecdotes in the context of a busy organisational setting.

Therefore, the fourth criterion is essential – your report has value to the extent that it can inform future actions (even if they are to replicate a successful campaign).

Most senior-level readers of this type of report will turn immediately to your recommendations. So don't treat it like a crime novel and build the suspense: start your report with your recommendations and then use your data and analysis to support them. This will compel you to be relevant in your selection of content. If you wish to summarise the findings in terms of success or not, two simple presentation tools create a compelling illustration of how your stakeholder engagement campaign has performed. Each borrows from powerful financial statements of performance, but please do not be seduced into thinking that their stakeholder audit equivalents are equally precise and quantifiable. Here, we are using them as a metaphor for performance.

Figure 9.9 below shows a stakeholder balance sheet and a stakeholder gains and losses statement. I recommend that you use one or the other rather than both.

A balance sheet provides a snapshot of the state of stakeholder engagement. The two sides need to balance of course, so the assets (positive, supportive stakeholders) match the work done, which includes the opening equity (stakeholders who were supportive at the outset). Likewise, the liabilities (stakeholders who oppose you or those who may turn away from you – contingent liabilities) are matched by the work you need to do and the time you need to invest in the engagement process.

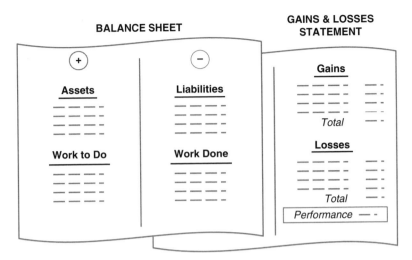

FIGURE 9.9 Two stakeholder engagement performance tools

On the gains and losses statement (profit seems an inappropriate term), you can demonstrate your performance over the last time period. The gains in terms of stakeholder support and assistance are weighed against the losses in terms of stakeholders who have turned against you or, worse, actively opposed you. You may want to evaluate a net position showing your overall performance as a net gain or loss.

Remember, these are compelling – even somewhat amusing – representations and cannot be truly quantitative. Do not try to make them so or you will be misrepresenting your evidence.

Learn

Following your audit and certainly at the end of your change programme, it is time to conduct a review of the lessons you and your team have learned. Do not just concentrate on the data, but engage your team members in a reflective process. Three good questions to ask are as follows:

- What ideas, contributions or events made the most difference to our stakeholder engagement?
- What were the most surprising events and outcomes?

- What would be your stakeholder engagement priorities on day one of a similar project?

What team members will most benefit from is an opportunity to consolidate the skills they have used and turn them into positive career and reputational assets. The biggest mistake people make in any kind of review is to focus on what went wrong. If you are familiar with the framework of 'Appreciative Inquiry', this is a good way to conduct your review.

In a nutshell, Appreciative Inquiry is a process of asking questions that uncover positive potential by finding and celebrating the best of what has happened. In this approach, the value of a lessons learned review is not in the neat document you produce at the end, but in the quality of the stories, folklore and rules of thumb that your experiences generate.

Whichever focus you put on your review, it is not so much what you do as how you do it. Aim to create a no-blame, no finger-pointing environment in which everyone has a say, is confident to speak out and is willing to learn. This is more important than any particular methodology or template. Do this by helping the group set ground rules that they are comfortable with and also by your own approach, including such basics as respectful behaviours, choice of language and tone of voice.

Embed

The reason to learn from your stakeholder engagement experiences is to create better engagement in the future, fully enrolling your stakeholders in the development and growth of your organisation and what it does. In the commercial world, this can deliver greater revenues, profitability and customer loyalty. For the non-profit sectors, you can deliver more appropriate services to higher standards. Let's end this chapter by considering how you can embed stakeholder engagement into the way your organisation operates.

Why would you create a positive stakeholder engagement culture?

A positive stakeholder engagement culture puts stakeholders at the forefront of all choices; it engages them in those choices and therefore benefits from higher levels of commitment and satisfaction. We examined, at the start of Chapter 1, the benefits of effective stakeholder engagement, but what are the benefits of embedding it into your culture?

- Continual and consistent levels of stakeholder feedback inform long-term decision-making.
- Prioritising stakeholder engagement will drive ethical practices and raise the social capital value of your organisation.
- Stakeholder engagement becomes a core skill, making more of your staff excellent practitioners.
- You have processes and systems that make results more predictable and easier to achieve. This is supported by robust documentation, tools and templates, and training packages.
- Staff have a shared language and methodologies to call upon, and levels of training and experience that will be valuable career assets.

What would a stakeholder engagement culture look like?

The details of a stakeholder engagement culture will look different in each organisation. It must mesh into an existing culture, will attend to different organisational priorities and will engage its own distinct ecosystem of stakeholders. However, some characteristics are generic. Let's look at how it will integrate with other areas of your culture.

Customer or client service

Almost certainly, a stakeholder-focused culture will place customers and clients at the forefront of your stakeholders, so how does this differ from a service-led culture? The answer lies in two words: context and balance. The 'customer is always right' culture that infuses many organisations can lead to resentment from staff. The most effective client or customer-facing organisations place customer service very clearly in the context of respect: we serve our customers because we want to and because it makes us feel good about ourselves. These organisations place staff equally at the heart of their business and this balance gives staff the desire to show why that is justified. A stakeholder-led approach creates a real balance among stakeholders whereby staff members cherish customers because the organisation cherishes all stakeholders.

Product or service development

Many fine companies begin their new product or new service development process by listening to 'the voice of the customer', placing client needs, and the problems they raise, at the start of the cycle. Increasing the range of stakeholders who are engaged in these early conversations can result in greater innovation and pre-empt problems later in the development process.

Management and leadership

Leadership at all levels will put a conspicuous emphasis on stakeholder engagement, prioritising it when allocating time in their schedule and making it an important part of their team management.

Policies and procedures

A strong culture does not arise from policies and procedures, but these are very distinctly a feature of that culture, creating consistency and identifying how engagement is managed and monitored at all levels, right up to the board, trustee or political level. Policies make engagement part of corporate governance and as such provide a powerful protection against ethical and reputational risks.

Competencies and capabilities

Culture cannot be taken for granted – especially as many organisations are being continually refreshed by in-flows and out-flows of staff. An initial cadre of trained and skilled practitioners needs to be supplemented by core training packages for large portions of the staff group, and competencies need to be locked into formal job descriptions and career progression frameworks. Continual sharing of lessons learned can further embed the culture, whilst building practical skills and situational-sensing capabilities.

Incentives and performance review

Extrinsic motivators like rewards and punishments are weak ways to build a culture, but do need to exist to strengthen the culture. What gets measured gets managed, so systems need to be in place to review stakeholder engagement performance and intelligent incentives need to drive choices that make stakeholder engagement a part of everyone's work.

Stakeholder engagement processes and tools

The whole culture needs to be underpinned by a reliable set of processes and tools, with supporting infrastructure and access to documentation, informal guidance and support from experienced colleagues.

How to create a stakeholder engagement culture

Achieving this ideal is not straightforward. I suggest the following six-step process.

Step 1: foundations

The first step is to examine the case for a stakeholder engagement culture in your business. Examine the evidence base for what is already being done and find good and bad practice benchmark comparisons in similar sectors. From this, build a business case that addresses costs as well as benefits.

Step 2: alignment

If you do not engage more than three-quarters of your senior leadership at the board (executives and non-executives) and second-tier levels, your initiative will be destined to fail. Use your business case from step 1 and tailor it to the needs of your stakeholders. Yes, practise what you are preaching and deliver great stakeholder engagement in your campaign to promote a stakeholder engagement culture. You must settle for nothing less than conspicuous support, a highly prominent sponsor, and allocation of sufficient funding and resources.

Step 3: definition

Now you have support and resources, you can start defining exactly what the term 'stakeholder engagement culture' means in your organisation. Once you have this, you can begin to develop the processes and tools that will support it. Make sure they are effective, but do not aim for perfect. The 80/20 rule should apply – look for the small proportion (say, 20 per cent) of tools that will deliver the majority (80 per cent, perhaps) of benefit. Develop working tools and prepare to pilot them. Use the pilot period to discover what works and how to improve your starter tools and processes. Also apply the 80/20 rule to the number of tools you develop. Avoid the temptation to specify too many tools – pick a small number that will be highly relevant to your context and focus on these.

Step 4: engagement

Now engage management at all levels – and staff too. You will need an enthusiastic cross-section of levels, skills and specialisms to pilot your processes and, here too, in enrolling your early supporters, you can be practising the engagement processes you have developed. Provide briefings and training, encourage ideas and contributions and, if possible, arrange visits to one or two reference organisations from whom team members can learn by observation and discussion with experienced practitioners.

Involve your early adopters in developing roll-out plans and testing tools, and ensure you provide them with first-class support mechanisms. Make excellent communication among this group – and from this group to the rest of the organisation – an early imperative.

Step 5: capability building

Now it is time to take the tools out for a test drive. Carefully select opportunities to demonstrate the value of the process and hone skills. Then communicate successes widely. From each opportunity, you should be able to enrol a few more supporters and advocates whom you can develop further with training. Now is your chance to start formalising your training materials into an established programme, with polished materials and case studies.

Step 6: evaluation

Recognise and celebrate the successes you are having and use both successes and setbacks as the basis for learning and honing approaches. Focus in particular on examples of excellence to learn from.

Now take what you have learned and re-engage, continuing the process, returning to step 4. Now you can evaluate pilot processes and tools, and develop them further. You can also test out your briefing and training materials.

Keep cycling around steps 4–6, growing the initiative each time, building towards the critical mass that will create a culture shift, but proving the value at each step along the way. Also continue to scan your business, political and competitive environments for changes that will have an impact on the tools and techniques you need to be developing and using. Start to embed evaluation and performance review into existing management and personnel processes.

The evolution of the culture: a stakeholder engagement maturity model

Software development, project management and risk management all have maturity models that set criteria to allow organisations to measure the level of institutionalisation of good practices. It is time that stakeholder engagement management also had a maturity model, so here is a proposal for a basic model. Others will doubtless be better qualified to develop this into a rigorous tool.

Table 9.1   Stakeholder engagement management maturity levels

Level 1 *Ad hoc*	No formal processes or recognition of the need for one. Any good work is done independently by individuals. Tools are shared informally among committed individuals and freely adapted, resulting in little or no uniformity.
Level 2 *Novice*	Awareness of the need for a systematic approach. Project and change management guidelines state requirements for stakeholder engagement management with little more than generic guidance and no substantial training available. Tools are 'home-made'.
Level 3 *Repeatable*	First documentation of stakeholder engagement policies and procedures is produced, with responsibilities allocated and some training available. People are aware of shortcomings and gaps. Simple tools are available centrally.
Level 4 *Managed*	Clear metrics are established to guide implementation and decision-making. Formal procedures are followed and individual levels of expertise are recognised, with formal training and development available. Sophisticated tools are available.
Level 5 *Embedded*	Stakeholder engagement is embedded in all organisational processes and is a part of the day-to-day culture. Knowledge, skills and techniques are constantly reviewed, with the organisation seen by others as a source of excellence and its senior practitioners regarded as leading experts.

A Call to Action

Project management is a mature discipline, supported by professional bodies, standards, extensive training resources and a huge literature. The same can increasingly be said for the newer, related disciplines of change management, programme management and portfolio management. One mark of their maturity is that component parts of these disciplines have become respected specialisms in their own right: estimating, planning and scheduling, resource management and risk management. In each of these areas, project managers have built up significant bodies of knowledge and toolsets, to the extent that experts can specialise and call themselves planners, resource managers and risk managers. I would like to see stakeholder engagement management join these specialisms. Like them, it is a crucial part of the success of any project or programme, there is a body of techniques and tools to learn and deploy, and it requires experience, skills and knowledge to do well.

Whether you share this ambition or not, what matters are the results you get and how you get them. I would like to see the methods and tools of stakeholder engagement become more than a short chapter in a project management book or a single exercise in a two-day training programme. I hope this book has shown you that there is more than enough material to allow project stakeholder engagement management to stand alone as a discipline with its own literature and toolset. And if it has, I would like to think that I have gone some way to creating a wider culture of effective and ethical stakeholder engagement within projects and programmes of change.

To everyone who aspires to engage respectfully with your stakeholders, or to manage that process, good luck.

Mike Clayton, March 2014

Appendix 1: Scenarios for the Influence Agenda

Business projects

- Intrapreneurial start-up
- New product/service launch
- Technology adoption
- Store refurbishment roll-out
- Technology refresh
- Office move
- Cost reduction
- Conference

Business transformation

- New business launch
- Take-over of another business
- Merger of broadly equal businesses
- Take-over by another business
- Management or employee buy-out
- Business unit sell-off
- Factory/warehouse/office closure
- Downsizing
- Relocation (new area)
- Re-organisation of departmental structure

Process change

- Regulatory compliance
- New factory process

- New appraisal process
- New expenses policy

Cultural transformation

- Increased focus on customer care
- Introducing performance measures
- Adoption of coaching culture
- Increasing innovation and creativity

Cyclical change

- Change of leadership
- Strategic planning process
- Annual budget negotiations
- New training programme

Community projects

- Development of a local plan
- New school, court building or hospital
- Town centre car park
- Traffic-calming measures

Governmental projects

- Consultation for new legislation
- Introduction of new legislation
- Establishing new executive function
- Spinning out an Executive Agency

Crises

- Natural disaster
- Environmental accident
- Accident involving serious injury or loss of life
- Product recall
- Data protection failure
- Legal or regulatory investigation
- Major industrial action

Appendix 2: Stakeholder List

Users/beneficiaries/customers/clients

1. Past customers (to whom you have ongoing obligations)
2. Past customers (to whom you have no formal ongoing obligations)
3. Current customers
4. Prospective customers
5. Client groups
6. Individual clients
7. Niche markets
8. Service users

Internal governance

9. The board
10. Trustees
11. Internal audit
12. Quality control
13. Health and safety
14. Fraud prevention

External governance/regulation

15. Government
16. Local government – metropolitan/unitary authority, county council, district/borough council, parish/town council
17. Regulators – e.g., health and safety, data protection, financial
18. Auditors
19. Standards assessors

Interest groups and influencers

20. Analysts
21. Customer representative groups
22. Consumer associations
23. User representative groups
24. Trades unions
25. Trade associations
26. Professional bodies
27. Other membership organisations
28. Non-governmental organisations
29. Pressure groups
30. Campaigning organisations
31. Individual activists
32. Political parties
33. Local politicians
34. National politicians
35. Business representatives – e.g., Institute of Directors, Confederation of British Industry, Chambers of Commerce

Partners

36. Business partners
37. Formal joint venture partners

Internal groups

38. Other projects
39. Internal communications/PR team
40. Accounts/finance department
41. HR/personnel department
42. New product development
43. Marketing
44. Sales
45. Catering
46. Manufacturing
47. Logistics and warehousing
48. Engineering
49. Maintenance
50. Facilities management
51. Customer service

52. Procurement
53. Operations
54. Research
55. Security

The public

56. The wider public
57. Your local community – residents
58. Your local community – business
59. Local schools
60. Universities and colleges
61. Local hospitals

Staff and owners

62. Shareholders
63. Investors
64. Pension funds
65. Owners
66. Senior executives
67. Your boss
68. Managers
69. Staff
70. Staff families
71. Retired staff
72. Former staff (alumni)
73. Pension fund members
74. Volunteers

Providers of goods and services

75. Suppliers
76. Lenders
77. Distributors/supply chain
78. Insurers
79. Consultants
80. Contractors
81. Subcontractors

82. Temps
83. Interims
84. Advisors
85. Utility suppliers – e.g., water, gas, electricity
86. Contract service suppliers – e.g., telecoms, Internet, transportation
87. Emergency services
88. Freeholder, head leaseholder

The environment

This is a list not of environmental pressure groups, which may be covered by items 27–33 above, but of aspects of the 'environmental stakeholder group':

89. Air/atmosphere
90. Farmland
91. Heathland
92. Forest and woodland
93. Coastal land
94. Parkland
95. Uplands and mountains
96. Rivers
97. Fisheries
98. Inshore seas
99. Open seas and oceans
100. Invertebrates
101. Fish
102. Reptiles and amphibians
103. Small mammals
104. Large native mammals
105. Birds
106. Farm animals
107. Trees
108. Other native plants and fungi
109. Future generations

Other

110. Competitors
111. The press and other media
112. Columnists and commentators

Note

While the distinctions between some of the examples (such as campaign groups and pressure groups) may seem fine or even non-existent, the existence of the different terms may mean you will find it easier to recognise examples in your own context from one label rather than the other.

Appendix 3: Additional Stakeholder Analysis Tools

Chapter 3 contains a basic set of stakeholder analysis tools that will serve you well in most circumstances. But special circumstances demand special tools, so this appendix lists an additional eight tools that you may want to use from time to time. Many are variants on the tools in Chapter 3, or on each other, but each difference may matter to you in understanding and presenting your information in the most helpful way possible.

Stakeholder interests map

Stakeholders each have a number of interests and concerns in a particular programme, and different stakeholders will have different, but overlapping, sets of interests. The stakeholder interests map allows you to visualise these interests, identify stakeholders who share particular interests and also spot those who have very similar profiles and may therefore be engaged within a single strategy. It can also help you to understand which interests dominate, which stakeholders are isolated and which minority interests you need to take account of. Each cell of the grid can either be ticked or left blank or, if you choose, different symbols can code for the level of interest (high, medium or low, for example, or different colours or shading options).

Template A.1   Stakeholder interests map

	Interest Areas				
Stakeholders	Strategic Direction	New Products	Factory Extension	Vehicle Access	Management Restructuring
The Board	High	Medium	High	Low	High
Staff and Managers	Medium	High	High	High	High
Customers	Medium	High	Low		Low
Local Residents			Medium	High	

Love-hate analysis

Most stakeholders do not have a simple polarity response to your project, either supporting it or opposing it. Instead, there are things that they like and support in what you are doing and there are things that they dislike and oppose. Some things have little or no interest to them. This can be a valuable analysis in discovering which topics to focus on to either strengthen relationships or mitigate threats.

Template A.2   Love-hate analysis

Stakeholder	Love	Don't Know/ Don't Care	Hate
The Board	Business plans	Extra traffic	Planning delays
Staff and Managers	Promotion prospects	–	Possible relocation
Customers	New products	Factory extension	Staff changes
Local Residents	Job opportunities	Business plans	Extra traffic

Salience map

Salience, or relevance, is a measure of how much a stakeholder stands out from the crowd and demands your attention. It therefore makes a strong measure of priority. Three things frequently combine to make a stakeholder stand out: power, legitimacy (how appropriate their involvement is) and urgency (the demands they make on your immediate attention). In Template A.3 below, we can classify stakeholders as falling into one of four boxes from high to low saliency, depending crudely on whether each of these three factors is high or low. You can adapt this methodology to your own measures of salience.

Template A.3   Salience map

Salience	Score	Stakeholders
Top Salience	↑P↑L↑U	
High Salience	↑P↑L↓U ↑P↓L↑U ↓P↑L↑U	
Low Salience	↑P↓L↓U ↓P↑L↓U ↓P↓L↑U	
Not Salient	↓P↓L↓U	

(continued)

Template A.3   Continued

Key			
↑P	High Power	↓P	Low Power
↑L	High Legitimacy	↓L	Low Legitimacy
↑U	High Urgency	↓U	Low Urgency

Stakeholder impact chart

The chart illustrated in Figure A.1 below allows you to visualise graphically the potential impact of stakeholders from the low-impact 'bystanders', who can do nothing but observe changes, to the high-impact 'transformers', who can potentially act as game changers, transforming what you are working on. The top half of the chart shows supportive stakeholders who are motivated to help you, whilst your critics, who may want to prevent your success, are at the bottom. In the figure, you can easily spot which stakeholders you already have a strong relationship with and which you do not.

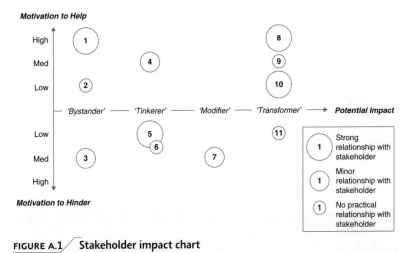

FIGURE A.1   Stakeholder impact chart

Power-interest diagram

This diagram is useful for a detailed look at a single stakeholder. It illustrates the sources of power a stakeholder has (their 'power bases') and their interests or concerns, towards which they will direct their power.

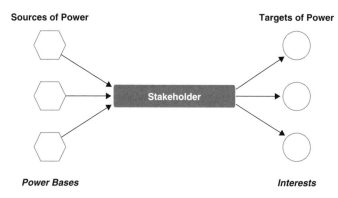

FIGURE A.2 / Power-interest diagram

Proximity map

If you want a simple way to visualise how close each of your stakeholders is to you or your project, the proximity map offers a simple solution. Define a few 'zones of proximity' (three to seven is about right) and then illustrate them as concentric circles, with the closest, most directly impacted stakeholders in the centremost ring and the most peripheral stakeholders in the outermost ring.

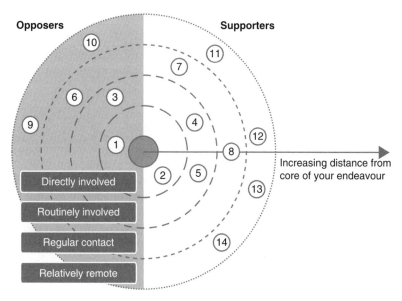

FIGURE A.3 / Proximity map

Relationship chart

In Chapter 3, we looked at sociograms as a way to map out relationships between stakeholders. You may simply want to focus on the strength of your relationship with each stakeholder. This differs from the proximity map, which effectively focuses on the level of interest rather than how well you are able to influence each stakeholder.

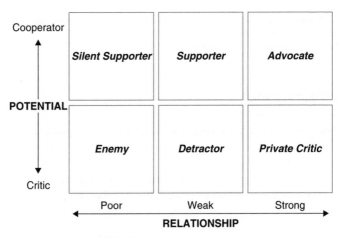

FIGURE A.4 Relationship chart

Interface network

Whilst sociograms focus on stakeholder relationships, you may simply be interested in the dependencies between stakeholders. For example, a utilities contractor will be dependent upon a local authority for consents and upon the health and safety team for approval to proceed. A builder will be dependent upon an architect for drawings, a building engineer for specifications and a subcontractor for some of the work. Each interface represents a dependency and each dependency represents a risk. So, typically, we would number them on the network to relate the dependencies to risks on our risk register.

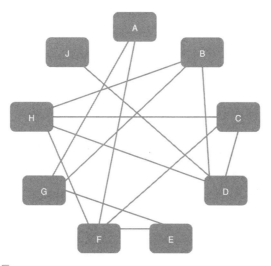

FIGURE A.5 **Interface network**

Appendix 4: Stakeholder Engagement Communication Methods

Formal	Informal
Face to face	*Face to face*
• Formal one-to-one • Seminars • Workshops • Town hall meeting • Presentations • Briefing • Training • Exhibitions • Conference • Roadshow • Surveys • Surgeries • Interviews • Focus groups	• Conversation • The 'grapevine' • Café conversations • Team meetings • Troubleshooting groups • Open days • Networking • Discussion groups
Distance	*Distance*
• Teleconferencing • Videoconferencing • Webinars • Video film	• Phone conversation • Text messaging
Written	*Written*
• Press pack/media briefing • Memos • Feedback forms • Questionnaires • Surveys • Email • Articles • Case studies • Reports	• Posters • Display boards • Text messages • Leaflets • FAQs

Online	*Online*
• Websites	• Blogs
• Webcasts	• Twitter, Yammer and similar
• Podcasts	micro-blogging tools
• Websites (public or intranet)	• Collaboration tools
• Online surveys	• YouTube
• Shared file space	• Online polls
• Workflow systems	• Discussion forums
• Wikis	• Forum posts
• RSS feeds	• Pinterest
• Secure collaboration tools	• Public social networks, e.g.,
• Discussion forums	Twitter, Facebook or LinkedIn
• Secure enterprise social networks, e.g., Yammer, Chatter, Convo or Tibbr	
Broadcast	*Broadcast*
• TV	• Newsletters
• Radio	• Bulletins
• Newspapers	• Website postings
• Magazines	
• Journals	
• In-house magazines	

Appendix 5: Ethical Stakeholder Engagement

A charter for ethical stakeholder engagement

First commitment: respect

1. To always respect all of your stakeholders.
2. To seek the insights and knowledge that your stakeholders possess, and to consider them objectively.
3. To assume the best of your stakeholders – in particular, that they act with positive intentions, even when their choice of behaviours is poor.
4. To allow your stakeholders to make their own decisions, free from any manipulation or coercion.

Second commitment: integrity

1. To always act with the utmost integrity.
2. To consider the consequences of your actions and take responsibility for your choices.
3. To be accountable for your actions to your stakeholders.
4. To act in good faith, refraining from acting solely in your own interests and, where they overlap with those of your stakeholders, to declare your interests openly.

Third commitment: equality

1. To disdain unethical discrimination of all kinds, respecting people for who they are rather than for the category into which they fall.
2. To offer or withhold no favour that is predicated upon either personal liking or animus.
3. To act in accordance with the basic human rights of each stakeholder.
4. To work towards a fair sharing of gains and losses among stakeholders.

Fourth commitment: minimise harm

1. To always act to safeguard the wider interests of your stakeholder group.
2. To strive to identify unintended consequences of your actions.
3. To balance with care the conflicting interests of different stakeholders, and to be open about the implications of those different interests.
4. To promote informed decision-making and to commit to facilitating the transparent processes and that will support it.

Fifth commitment: tell no lies

1. To always remember that honesty is the only ethical policy.
2. To present the whole truth, bad as well as good, and to tell only the truth.
3. To avoid deliberately exaggerating, diminishing, omitting or selectively interpreting the evidence.
4. To let your stakeholders know all of the consequences of the choices they might make, including the adverse ones.

Sixth commitment: honour the rules

1. To always act in accordance with laws, regulations and rules that are imposed through due process, whether by nations, states, administrative regions or the organisations to which you are bound.
2. To respect contractual commitments that you and your stakeholders have made or that have been made by organisations to which you or your stakeholders are bound.
3. To meet the requirements of all properly appointed people who have been assigned seniority over you by the organisations to which you are bound.
4. To remain mindful that your ethical and moral duties can sometimes transcend points 1, 2 and 3 of the sixth commitment, and that you are, at all times, responsible for your choices.

I freely make these commitments on this day: . . . . *Date* . . . .

Signed: . . . .

Appendix 6: Rules, Rules, Rules

If you like the stakeholder engagement rules spread throughout this book, here they are, gathered together, along with a few others. A total of ten seems a good number!

Stakeholder Rule Number 1

Your stakeholders will determine the success, or not, of your project.

Stakeholder Rule Number 2

Projects and change would be easy if it were not for the people involved.

Stakeholder Rule Number 3:

Honesty is not the best policy … it is the only policy.

Stakeholder Rule Number 4:

Communicate with people in the way that they like to communicate.

Stakeholder Rule Number 5, the Golden Rule of Resistance:

Always respect your resisters.

Stakeholder Rule Number 6

Tomorrow's leaders are today's juniors.

Stakeholder Rule Number 7

You can never communicate enough …
until the point where you have communicated too much!

Stakeholder Rule Number 8

If you want to be right all the time …
you have to be prepared to change your mind quickly.

Stakeholder Rule Number 9

> *Never say anything <u>about</u> someone that you would not be prepared to say <u>to</u> them.*

Stakeholder Rule Number 10

> *Never assume that your stakeholders play by the same rules as you do.*

Appendix 7: Selected Glossary

Affect: the word psychologists use for our emotional state.

Apex stakeholders: stakeholders who can influence many other stakeholders, but are little influenced by other stakeholders around them. They are hard to influence, but can create a lot of leverage if you can do so.

Appreciative Inquiry (AI): a process of asking questions that uncover positive potential by finding and celebrating the best of what has happened. AI uncovers stories, folklore and rules of thumb that your experiences create, to design practical solutions to organisational challenges.

Attitude: the emotional state that accompanies the stakeholder's interest or concern.

Balanced scorecard: the old adage is 'what gets measured gets managed'. A balanced scorecard creates measures across a range of different criteria to ensure that the work you are doing does not disproportionately focus on some of your objectives at the cost of others.

Basal stakeholders: stakeholders who have changeable views and are easily influenced, and so tend to go with the flow of opinion.

Behavioural economics: a theory of decision-making that starts from the position that human behaviour is often irrational, yet it is largely predictable if we can gather enough social, emotional and cognitive data.

Benefits register: a tool that provides a detailed schedule of all of the positive outcomes designed into the programme.

Bystanders: low-impact stakeholders who can do nothing but observe changes.

Choice architecture: within the discipline of 'behavioural economics', how we ask questions and set up situations will determine the choices people make.

The Clarkson Principles: a set of seven principles of stakeholder management set out by Max Clarkson, an important early thinker about business ethics and stakeholder theory. They were drafted with corporate social responsibility in mind and apply across all business processes. In Appendix 5, I have provided my own set of six commitments for ethical stakeholder engagement in the form of a charter.

Coercive power: the power organisations have over their stakeholders when they are prepared and able to command and control them using strong incentives and disincentives to enforce the desires of the owners.

Confirmation bias: the tendency to focus on information that confirms what we already believe to be true and, consequently, to screen out contradictory evidence.

Deming Cycle: the common name for what W. Edwards Deming himself referred to as the Shewhart Cycle, the fundamental control cycle in industrial processes, first introduced by Walter Shewhart: plan-do-study-act.

Deontology: the study of what is morally necessary or forbidden.

Early adopters: a term coined by Everett Rogers in his theory of the diffusion of innovations for highly influential stakeholders, who embrace a change early – but not first. Early adopters are socially connected and respected, and therefore easily become opinion leaders. They may well become 'apex stakeholders'.

Econs: a term coined by Richard Thaler for near-mythical people who behave wholly rationally, according to the assumptions of early economic theory.

Empty the hopper: a process of calmly, patiently and respectfully eliciting every objection that a stakeholder has and dealing with it. When there are no more objections, the hopper is empty and any remaining objection is purely emotional.

Floating voter: a stakeholder who has not made up their mind as to whether they will support or oppose your project.

Frame: the context in which a problem will be solved or a decision made.

Heuristics: the mental simplifications and shortcuts that we use to find answers and make choices.

Hidden power: the ability to influence the choices that 'System 1' makes.

Hofstadter's Law: a law proposed by Douglas Hofstadter – 'It always takes longer than you expect, even when you take into account Hofstadter's Law.'

Impact: the ability to affect the realities of the world through power or influence.

Influence: the ability to affect other people's attitudes and behaviours.

Intelligent persistence: the quality of keeping working at something important, but in a way that constantly reviews the efficacy of what you are doing and makes adjustments accordingly.

Interest: the level of concern with the project.

Knowing-doing gap: the difference between learning something and being able to do it.

Marginal stakeholder: a stakeholder who is neither for you nor against you – either because they are truly neutral or because they are undecided.

Microscope objections: objections that focus on tiny details and specific concerns.

Monitor and control loop: observe – interpret – intervene.

Neutral stakeholder: a stakeholder who is undecided about an issue.

Normative power: the ability to secure compliance through shared beliefs and values. Organisations in the voluntary, campaigning and caring sectors wield this power.

Nudge: a situation or circumstance that predictably shifts behaviours whilst retaining total freedom of choice.

The onion model of resistance: my basic model of how stakeholders resist change. It is constructed in layers of resistance, each successive one getting hotter and more uncomfortable to deal with.

Outlier stakeholder: a stakeholder whom most people would fail to notice as having a stake.

Perceptual positions: we can see the world from our own point of view, that of the person we are dealing with or from a neutral, third party perspective. These are the perceptual positions and form a good basis to understand a stakeholder and plan how to engage them.

Persona: a realistic representation of a fictional character who is typical of a stakeholder group, often based on real data from demographic and survey information, coupled with knowledge from focus groups, online behaviours, interviews and sometimes informed speculation.

Political: relating to the complex set of relationships among people and groupings within a culture, society or organisation, often involving the exercise of authority or power.

Power: the ability to impose your will over people or events.

Power base: a source of social power. John French and Bertram Raven identified seven; other commentators have added more.

Primary stakeholder: a stakeholder who is readily influenced by others (unlike 'apex stakeholders'), but not necessarily by an apex stakeholder. They are good at influencing others and can therefore have a significant impact on perceptions.

Secondary stakeholder: a stakeholder who is readily influenced by 'apex and primary stakeholders'. They have an important role to play in the project and may have limited influence over others.

Shewhart Cycle: a fundamental control cycle in industrial processes, first introduced by Walter Shewhart: plan-do-study-act.

Sociogram: sometimes called a 'social network diagram', a simple way to map relationships among stakeholders.

Soft power: the ability to attract, co-opt and persuade.

Stakeholder: anyone who has any interest in what you are doing.

Stakeholder engagement: the process of actively contacting, communicating with and influencing a stakeholder.

Stakeholder engagement audit: a structured review of your 'stakeholder engagement' processes and implementation, against pre-determined objectives, to measure effectiveness and identify lessons to be learned and implemented.

Stakeholder engagement culture: an organisational culture that places effective, respectful 'stakeholder engagement' at the heart of processes, systems, decision-making and problem solving.

Stakeholder engagement management: managing the 'stakeholder engagement' process.

Stakeholder management: the process of influencing stakeholders to further the objectives of your organisation, programme or project. This book prefers the term 'stakeholder engagement' and the distinction is one of tone, engagement implying a more respectful and less manipulative approach, with longer-term goals, less about the mechanics of communicating and more about building and nurturing productive, mutually beneficial relationships.

Stakeholder map: one of many tools that represents stakeholders' characteristics in a visual format.

Stakeholder triage: a quick evaluation of a range of stakeholders against a small number of highly salient criteria to sort them into groups that will help in prioritising which stakeholders to engage with most actively.

Sticky: a term coined by Chip and Dan Heath, characterising communications that are readily understood and remembered, and that have a lasting impact.

Swift trust: a process that accelerates the creation of trust between you and your stakeholder.

System 1 and System 2: terms relating to two distinct ways we process information mentally. System 1 is a fast, automatic process that draws on experience and intuition, requiring relatively little energy. It can be irrational and prone to bias. System 2 represents our slower, more deliberate, analytic thinking process.

Telescope objections: objections that are often so broad and unspecific that you cannot get a clear understanding of what they are and how to respond fully to them.

Transformers: the high-impact stakeholders who can potentially act as game changers, transforming what you are working on.

Utilitarian power: the power wielded by organisations that exchange rewards for compliance, establishing a trading relationship with their employees.

Appendix 8: Learn More: Bibliography

Ansoff, H. Igor (1965). *Corporate Strategy*. McGraw-Hill.

Ariely, Dan (2009). *Predictably Irrational: The Hidden Forces that Shape Our Decisions*. HarperCollins.

Beach, Lee Roy (1997). *The Psychology of Decision-Making: People in Organizations*. SAGE Publications, Inc.

Carnegie, Dale (2006). *How to Win Friends and Influence People*, new edn. Vermillion.

Cialdini, Robert B. (2008). *Influence: The Science and Practice*, 5th edn. Pearson.

Clayton, Mike (2010). *The Handling Resistance Pocketbook*. Management Pocketbooks.

——. (2010). *How to Speak so People Listen*. Pearson

——. (2011). *Brilliant Influence*. Pearson.

——. (2011) *Risk Happens! Managing Risk and Avoiding Failure in Business Projects*. Marshall Cavendish.

Deci, Edward (1997). *Why We Do What We Do*, reprint edn. Penguin.

Dutton, Kevin (2011). *Flipnosis: The Art of Split-Second Persuasion*. Arrow.

Fisher, Roger and Ury, William (2012). *Getting to Yes: Negotiating an Agreement without Giving in*. Random House Business.

Freeman, R. Edward (2010) *Strategic Management: A Stakeholder Approach*. Cambridge University Press.

Gardner, Howard (2004). *Changing Minds: The Art and Science of Changing Our Own and Other People's Minds*. Harvard Business School Press.

Heath, Chip and Heath, Dan (2008). *Made to Stick*. Arrow.

Hofstadter, Douglas R. (2000). *Gödel, Escher, Bach: An Eternal Golden Braid*, 20th anniversary edn. Penguin.

Hogan, Kevin (2004). *The Science of Influence: How to Get Anyone to Say Yes in 8 Minutes or Less!* John Wiley & Sons.

Kahneman, Daniel (2012), *Thinking, Fast and Slow*. Penguin.

Kaplan, Robert S. and Norton, David P. (2005). 'Balanced Scorecard: Measures that Drive Performance'. *Harvard Business Review*, July.

Kramer, Roderick M. and Tyler, Tom R. (1996). *Trust in Organizations*. SAGE Publications, Inc.

Lewis, Sarah (2011). *Positive Psychology at Work: How Positive Leadership and Appreciative Inquiry Create Inspiring Organizations*. Wiley-Blackwell.

Lewis, Sarah, Passmore, Jonathan and Cantore, Stefan (2011). *Appreciative Inquiry for Change Management: Using AI to Facilitate Organizational Development*. Kogan Page.

Lowndes, Leil (2008). *How to Talk to Anyone: 92 Little Tricks for Big Success in Relationships*. Thorsons.

Maurer, Rick (2010). *Beyond the Wall of Resistance: Why 70% of All Changes Still Fail – And What You Can Do About it*, revised 2nd edn. Bard Press.

Merrill, David W. and Reid, Roger H. (1981). *Personal Styles & Effective Performance*. CRC Press.

Nye, Joseph S. (1991). *Bound to Lead: The Changing Nature of American Power*, new edn. Basic Books.

——. (2005). *Soft Power: The Means to Success in World Politics*, new edn. Public Affairs, U.S.

Packard, Vince (2007). *The Hidden Persuaders*, reissue edn. Ig Publishing.

Patterson, Kerry, Grenny, Joseph, Maxfield, David, Mcmillan, Ron and Switzler, Al (2007). *Influencer: The Power to Change Anything*. McGraw-Hill Professional.

Perloff, Richard M. (2013). *The Dynamics of Persuasion: Communication and Attitudes in the 21st Century*, 5th edn. Routledge.

Pink, Daniel (2011). *Drive*. Cannongate Books Ltd.

Rogers, Everett M. (2003). *The Diffusion of Innovations*, 5th edn. Free Press.

Thaler, Richard H. and Sunstein, Cass R. (2009). *Nudge: Improving Decisions About Health, Wealth and Happiness*. Penguin.

Titmus, Richard M. (1997). *The Gift Relationship: From Human Blood to Social Policy*. New Press.

Appendix 9: Hear Mike Clayton Speak about *The Influence Agenda*

Mike is a conference speaker and business consultant. He speaks at conferences, team events, workshops and seminars for companies, associations, public authorities and not-for-profit organisations.

Mike's topics include project management and the management of change, advanced communication, management and leadership, wisdom and personal effectiveness.

If you want to spread the Influence Agenda within your organisation, Mike is available for speaking engagements, seminars and training and, with the publisher, can offer special deals on bulk purchases of this book.

You can book Mike to talk about the Influence Agenda or another topic at: www.mikeclayton.co.uk or www.theinfluenceagenda.co.uk.

Appendix 10: Also by Mike Clayton

Mike Clayton is author of 11 other books to date.

How to Manage a Great Project
On Budget, On Target, On Time
Pearson, 2013

How to Speak so People Listen
Grab Attention, Hold it, and Get Your Message Across
Pearson, 2013

The Yes/No Book
How to Do Less... and Achieve More
Pearson, 2012

Smart to Wise
The Seven Pillars for True Success
Marshall Cavendish, 2012

Brilliant Project Leader
What the Best Project Leaders Know, Do and Say to Get Results, Every Time
Pearson, 2012

Brilliant Stress Management
How to Manage Stress in Any Situation
Pearson, 2011

Risk Happens!
Managing Risk and Avoiding Failure in Business Projects
Marshall Cavendish, 2011

Brilliant Time Management
What the Most Productive People Know, Do and Say
Pearson, 2011

Brilliant Influence
What the Most Influential People Know, Do and Say
Pearson, 2011

The Handling Resistance Pocketbook
Management Pocketbooks, 2010

The Management Models Pocketbook
Management Pocketbooks, 2009

Who Else Needs *The Influence Agenda?*

Just about everyone in business, public service or the voluntary and charitable sector needs to influence in a sustained and ethical manner. Who do you know that is working hard to create worthwhile change or in the planning stages of a significant project?

Why not do them a favour, call, email or tweet them today about *The Influence Agenda*. Who knows, it may just transform the way they engage their stakeholders and bring them better results. What better way can there be to strengthen your relationship in under a minute?

Contact Mike or the publishers, Palgrave Macmillan, to enquire about orders of *The Influence Agenda* for your whole team.

mike@mikeclayton.co.uk
orders@palgrave.com

Index

Printed and bound by CPI Group (UK) Ltd, Croydon, CR0 4YY